ASCENSIONS REIGN

Where Did You Put Your Pain God?!

DR. CATHLEEN M. SCHMITT

ISBN-13: 978-1548765224

ISBN-10: 1548765228

DEDICATION

This book is dedicated to Jesus Christ. He is the only one I know who had the power over the darkness within me. He then went into the infernal regions within my being, and rescued my heart from its self-imposed hell. Bringing my heart to rest in His heart, I now lean into His name and walk in Divine favor and health.

It is also dedicated to my Mother, my dearest friend and cheerleader. You died suddenly; just months shy of this being finished. Your legacy of courage and love live in these pages and in all of our hearts. It's done Mom! How I love you.

CONTENTS

Part one – Where Did You Put Your Pain God?!

Part Two – Where Did You Put Your Reign Lord?

ACKNOWLEDGMENTS & THANK YOU!

Thank you first, to my Lord and King, Savior and friend, **Jesus Christ**.

Thank you to **Ian Clayton** who helped me to understand the language of the Lord in my life, even though that language is in pictures and visions. For almost 20 years you have given me keys and strategies to unlock the reason and purpose for this sight. You have led me to His heart, chambers, courts and realms and, in doing so, I am now more alive as a spirit being, instead of only a human being. Gen 1: 26 God said, "Let us make man in our image and likeness." Thus, I was created a spirit, with a soul, housed in a body. As my spirit, soul, and body came into the rule of the Kingdom of God within, it showed in the rule of heaven outwards in all my circumstances – on earth as it is in heaven.

A special thank you to **Nancy Coen** . She carries the sounds of God Almighty. which then released my mind and physical body. .as the Holy Spirit bore me up ,in my weakness.. with sounds that could not be uttered.. true.. but they could be whistled.. hummed.. vibrated and sung.. Without you Nancy.. I would never of known how to SOUND BACK to my God.. and King. .in love.. Through three days of horrendous withdrawals.. as drugs went out of my body.. and brain.. God Sounded back to my Spirit.. and my body had to obey. I love you with my whole heart in His.. sincerely, Dr. Cathleen.

To **Ambassador Clyde Rivers**, who for nearly eleven years now, has stood as my Pastor and friend. Your conviction that the traditions of man make the word of God null and void, changed my life, and I could not take the grace of God as an excuse to sin anymore. You gave me the Word to hear God's instruction, then gave me the freedom to hear His voice. Through many trials of faith, you counseled, contended and comforted me, till God's voice within me, and your words around me, often became one and the same. Now to the increase of God's government and peace we stand; till one Nation under God with Liberty and Justice for all, is a fact once again!

To my three sons: **Lawrence**, **Stephen**, and **Gary Jr. Schmitt**, it was often with your blood on my pen that this book was written as my mind became whole in God. You each love and serve Him deeply, for this I am truly thankful, and can truly be called your mother, not just a friend. Sarah, you married Lawrence and have become so strong in love and wisdom. I am in awe of you. You are my daughter in every sense of the word. Nicole, thank you for taking on our grandbabies as your own, and bring us a new one in just a couple weeks. Your faith will keep you.

To the Father of our children, Gary Sr., Thank you.

To Jack and Tina Schmitt, my brother and sister in law: I would not be alive if it were not for both of you. The depth of love and character it took to stay faithful in this journey is truly a miracle. Tina, you are a deep angel-engaging woman of faith. Jack, you are a sincere, loving man of integrity and grit...love you.

To my brothers and sisters: Cindy, you never left me and always heard my cry. Michael, you were the only male in my life that showed true godly love. Chrissy, you held me as a nurse, a sis, and a teacher. Then you said, "Okay now, finish it." Brian, your straight-gut, core belief in God is a fresh breeze in a sea of fake faces. Barry, as Mom died it was you who brought me out of shock. With your gentle fierceness, I caught my breath. You have the heart of a grizzly! Ben, excellence, wisdom and a child-like faith, a potent balance of a real man of honor. And Ceil, your passion and guts gave me courage to believe God out of addiction. You rescued me when I was in deep trouble, and stood even when, in my own eyes, I could not. You are so strong. I love you.

Sylvia you have great faith to carry on even when it would be easier at times to give in. Vicky, you are faithful and brilliant. I love you and miss your face. Terri and Mark, I hope to know you more and more.

I give a special thank you to my niece, Annette Harkins. Just two months after my healing and cure my brother called, "Hey Cath, can you talk to Annette?" She needs to talk to someone." I spoke to a post-suicide-attempted, broken, fractured wild animal inside. Wild-hearted yet wounded, childlike yet, desperate. Hmmm, I had nothing. Yet I knew HIM; God. I did two years of raw, gut-wrenching, soul-searching questioning and demanded answers. And "Don't just tell me it will be okay with Annette!" Why? How? Show me! Who? Angels and light, Gods very light, tears and fears gave way to cheers and hope. And very slowly, love won as the journey continued. I'm not sure which one was the teacher, and which the student. God taught us both and today we stand in Him, my niece and daughter. Now we are strong, sober and free to love and be and breathe.

To Doctor Robin Lococo: Thank you for your heart in the midst of truth, administration and life. Your expectations of integrity and honor and the ability to rule while still understanding weakness, is amazing. Through leaning into worship and the Word, you are an example of integrity in my life. Thank you.

To my editors:

Valerie Stripe: You took the roughest draft and made it intelligible. Thank you for grace, grace, grace!

Pastor Cheri and Carey: Your hours of typing and taking what would seem like drug-induced hallucinations into stunning, deep revelations of a Loving God!

To Jayme: Your selfless hours brought it up to code.

And last, but far from least, to Starlett Hovious who inserted chapters, and finished the outside coverings. Your deep heart to mother and corral this wild heart into a table of His contents is truly a miracle of God.

DR. CATHLEEN M. SCHMITT

FOREWORD

The focus of this book is to introduce the Law of the Spirit of Life in Christ Jesus as a governing standard that has turned my spirit, body and soul from the Law of Sin and Death. KJV Rom 8: 2, Malachi 4: 6

Two years ago, July and August of 2012, my dearest friend Jayme flew me to her house. For nearly 6 weeks I was caught up in a physical and spiritual encounter inside the beating stripes and pierced body of Jesus Christ. I was also caught up into the courts of Heaven. I have walked pain free and physically strong since then... including canceling even another total knee replacement in August of 2012. At 56 years old, I climb mountains, walk miles and am as fit as a 30 year old.

It is there, inside of Christ's body and the courtroom that I learned that there is a rule above the earth, yet inside of Christ, in me. The Law of the Spirit of Life in Christ Jesus that goes above pain, above emotional trauma, above in love--that has made me free from sin and death in my body, soul, and spirit.

Now, I hated laws. I was told to calm down, take your medications, do this, and do that, breathe in, breathe out, from every doctor counselor and authority known. Law?!? No, thank you! Even in God, I didn't need any more law; not me. Laws are for 'them', because I'm special and I'm different. Truthfully, I was isolated and with unbalanced emotional excuses and responses. I was a law unto myself. So, a law of the Spirit of Life, what could this possibly do? What it does through this book, through my life, through Christ, is give me a fixed position and breath to fully live in the necessary power of the government of and the King's domain, Kingdom of God within, and the Kingdom of heaven throughout.

It is a law of love that would not change with circumstances, or emotional highs and lows. Immutable, God ordained, and is able to defy the law of sin and death in my body soul and spirit, and thus my circumstances. This, then, set me free from condemnation, which is the lesser, lower law of sin and death. (K.J.V Romans 8: 2) "For the law of the Spirit of life in Christ Jesus, hath made me free from the law of sin and death."

INTRODUCTION

This book, my life in Christ, takes my heart, separated from God, from His love into the various levels of acceptance of His love. It is proof that through the valley of the shadow of death (Psalm 23), that God's revelation begins and ends through the heart, thus the mind can be healed, won and wooed to perfection in Him.

In the midst of physical and mental pain, God's word, God Himself, is the only factor that never changes. Pain revealed itself to me early in my life. Through God, I now know it is only a fallen angel disguised as a messenger of God. Pain offers misery suffering and brokenness as false badges of honor. Imposters in a twisted, self-absorbed, self-centered pity party, in which I hourly attended. Story after dreadful story came forth... "Oh, my back was so much sorer today. I tried everything, but God really came through in the end. Oh my foot just ached, but God helped me to see, eventually. Oh the terrible pounding in my head. After trying over the counter drugs, warm washcloths and a heating pad, all to no avail, but God came and gave me grace."

But God, but God, but God... God is not the "but" of any statement. He is not an added ingredient when everything else fails. He is, however Wonderful, Counselor, Mighty God, Everlasting Father, and Prince of Peace: and of the increase of His government and peace there shall be no end. Isaiah 9:6-7 He caused me to rely on Him as these descriptions of Him state, and thus I know a Counselor within my own core. I know a Daddy, everlasting, who will not beat or belittle me because I need Fatherly comfort. Peace, Might and Wonder are just names compared to the holding, safe, merciful strength revealed to my heart, even in the heat of my heart's rebellion.

I had no set rule inside my own heart. I was always excused by another illness or another medication. "Oh that's just the way Cathy is," many would say. However this statement was the killer dismissal of responsibility to me or for the result of my actions. With my mind always betraying my heart, I expressed a poem:

How betrayal's blade must have shorn into twisted shreds all hope of love. In a kiss; in a Judas kiss, therein lies a weapon sharper than any created.

An enemy's spear would have sweetened the blow, for weapons pierce only flesh, yet this, this inward betrayal bleeds out my heart, my chest.

Oh Father, oh God, take this, yet not my will but Thine be done.

Now, one might ask, "Fine, you talk to God?" Yes. He speaks to me in visions, encounters and walking with Him. This is not because I was anything special, it is because He is. The pathways to get information to my mind were blocked. I could not remember spoken words for very long, nor count on feelings that changed with the wind. But pictures, photos, OHHHH yes! I loved taking pictures and still do, more than anything else. God created me, so He knew the only way I would remember Him was through the picture language. This way, no matter if I was an addict or an animal, a person or a prescription, one thing always remained, the images of Him. Soon the images His Word produced in my being were more powerful than the false pictures and images I had been led to believe about myself.

Now one may ask, "I don't even know how to talk to God. Where do you begin, even if I wanted to?" This is a very profound and awesome question. In fact, this question was even asked by Jesus' disciples in Matthew 6. They asked Lord teach us to pray. Pray = speech, communication with God. So this is an excellent question. Jesus also answers them in the same chapter. His answer begins; "Our Father who art in heaven." Our Father? I am supposed to address him as a Father? I don't think so! My dad was not someone I could talk to. I longed for a father that would sit with me and tell me that I am good and beautiful. Didn't happen. NO thank you!

This is true for many of my friend also. So as I questioned this answer, the Lord said "Look, look closer. It says our Father who art in heaven. In heaven. Heaven is above evil. Heaven is good. So what, Cath, did you want in a father? What did you need? Take an empty chair, place it beside where ever you want to talk to him and tell 'our Father' what you need. Tell him it would have been awesome to go fishing. It would have been wonderful to dance with him at your wedding. It would be nice if he protected me, held me or was strong for me when I couldn't be. It would have been nice if he would have just been a safe place to be weak." So I poured out my heart to this empty chair for days and days. Soon the chair was not so empty any more, in my room and in my heart.

I wasn't the only one talking; He was and that's all I know. We would talk for hours and walk in His heavenly images and places. As I began to trust in Him. He showed me that there IS NO PAIN OR SHAME SO DEEP, THAT HIS LOVE IS NOT DEEPER STILL.

So, come away now. The first chapter is about to begin. It ends in a very sweet loving encounter. If this is boring, that is ok, skip it. Yet in order to know the answer of the cry of my broken being, I had to be reminded of all that was safe, in Him.

He had to remind me of Himself in the beginning, for God is love. If the beginning and the end of the matter does not lead you to love in Him and others more, then it is nothing. 1 Corinthians 13.

PART ONE

Where Did You Put Your Pain God?!

DR. CATHLEEN M. SCHMITT

1

LOVE'S BASE

"She" sits on her friend Jayme's couch, screaming loudly in hopeless agony. Broken, addicted, in pain and fear, she screams from the core of her being, "Help me!" In ravaged agony of pain's price and addiction's control, she pleads to the only One who can answer her, and has answered her, with thoughts, dreams and visions. He has answered her in love, yet she does not recognize His love in her body's broken, fractured state. Sobbing, soaked and desperate, wracked in the physical pain from a car accident and too many surgeries to remember, too many pills to count, and too much pain to just 'have faith'; she is blinded.

"Oh Lord!" she bewails. "Where did You put Your Pain? Where did You put Your pain?" Without having this answer, she knows she will over-dose and die, she knows it deep inside.

"Why is my pain perpetual and my wound incurable, refusing to be healed?" (KJV, Jeremiah 15:18) With her muscles cramping, head pounding, always pounding, craving to be stilled for just another minute, just another pill to shut up her body's demands, dark tormenting driving fears; she can't go through withdrawals. More pills equal less pain. Fear escalates until it is time for another refill. She must keep on... at all cost. Withdrawal means endless days of

1

shaking, throwing up, inside-out itching in every cell and muscle like bugs crawling out with insane itching that can't be scratched. No! So she must control it all; pain, pills, life. Relief is never fully realized. There is always the driving need to be "okay" or else "they" may see her weakness and put her away. And yet, somehow God still finds a way to answer her, to remind her, to cause her to remember... to remember that God is love.

"I learned to get by without allowing anyone or anything to touch this place in the core of my being."

God is love and I (the author of this book), am the "she". I am writing this book as a tribute and "thank you" to the Lord. In August of 2002, I was in a car accident that jammed my body and rocked my soul. In the valley of this shadow of death and pain I discovered the physical pain that I experienced actually revealed my heart pain that had been masked all too long. The pain of my heart was not being able to accept being loved, truly loved, for love to me had become too painful.

I learned to get by without allowing anyone or anything to touch this place in the core of my being. The good in me soon was overrun by the physical pain, surgeries, abuse and guilt. Questions constantly bombarded my mind: "If they only knew this place where you have to take drugs. If they only knew that you're numb inside. If they only knew that you walk and talk with God... and yet you are so physically broken, they would get rid of, reject or dismiss you!"

So, I learned to separate my sweet, good, loving child heart from the all-knowing, people-pleasing adult(s). Yet as was written so long ago, "A house divided against itself cannot stand." (KJV, Mark 3:25) Before the kingdom of God's love healed my body, soul, and spirit, many would say of me: "Oh, she's 'seeing' again. Too bad her body is still broken. She is a little off ya know, just another way of escaping what's really going on. She's harmless, thank God! Loving, oh, so loving, but clueless... maybe one day she will wake up and not spend so much time 'up there' with Him." Yet "up there" was where the core of my heart was safe. My mind was injured, but oh, how my heart did see!

Even as a little child, before I could speak, I knew of Jesus. My mother made sure of that by taking me to church! At seven, I had my first Holy Communion. It is then that I became aware that Jesus was more than a name. He visited me in my dreams, in my heart. I focused on our daily encounters, the dreams, pictures and visions of Him became normal to me. Gardens, rivers and wonders revealed, became a language between us, God and I, a panorama, which I enjoyed, that carried me away, far away, yet were so real compared to life at home. So, to answer my paralyzing plea of dark ravaged hurt, He speaks to me in our language of visions, pictures and dreams. "Where did You put Your pain?" Before He could fully answer me, He caused me to remember how much He loved me; to remember our language of love.

In my heart the good, loving "Jesus Cathy" would receive His picture language, and as I learned to turn my thoughts to this place, I would be caught up into amazing encounters.

"Before He could fully answer me, He caused me to remember how much He loved me; to remember our language of love."

Beautifully so! For years I'd been able to remember Him; His garden, His smile, and every other stress or responsibility would be gone. This is okay at first – for a child. But ultimately, as I would come to know He is God, not an escape hatch.

"Where did your put your pain God?" cries to be answered. So He takes me in pictures and visions first to His heart of Love. His Word. His heartbeat. He assures me my answer will come, has come, and beckons me to come away. Yet, not just a random "out there" experience, He takes me "up" by taking me in... into the chambers of the heart of His word. First, the chambers of love, which eventually become known as the Judge's chambers of Love's law, all in the heart of His living Word. "Remember Cath. Remember Me, for unless you remember our very base of love, the answer to your pleas about pain will not stand. So now, for a moment, come away with Me to beauty. Remember, remember, remember... Me." I respond to His beckoning and ponder Psalm 23. Vision:

"The Lord is my shepherd; I shall not want. He makes me to lie down in green pastures; He leads me beside the still waters..." (KJV, Psalm 23:1-2) Still waters – as I lean my thoughts towards this verse my natural eyes close. The eyes of my heart open and I allow myself to be wooed by the sound of His Word, His love, His flow inside of me... "Rest now Cathy. Just be and breathe, be and breathe." Earthly cares and questions fade as my focus comes away into His Word. He makes me to lie in fresh green pastures, green pastures. I see before me fields of splendor with towering purple blooms and honeycomb blossoms. Lilacs lace a path so clear. Colorful ladybugs seem to catch my stare – "Come closer now, come, come." I do not have to move. My desire to simply have a closer look, a deeper smell, propels me forward. Thought is action and desire done.

Everything is so alive, as am I. The fragrance of this field of splendor surrounds me, yet it is also somehow in me and on me. I'm a part of the very core and the very scent of the towering lilacs, fragrant and free, bending with each breeze. The ground beneath me is also alive with grass that cushions yet somehow urges me onward – to find the water, the still waters. The grass bends without crushing and I want to lie down for just a moment, a precious moment to just be and breathe. I pause and reflect on how truly I am one with every living thing. A harmony deep inside unites grass and flowers and trees into a sound deep within my being. Yet, even in this moment of bliss, the hum of the waters and the harmony of all creation draws me; woos me.

There's more than this, there's more. So, by a universal call, I am ushered through the various wonders of marigolds, mums, and flowers so tall – like white iridescent walls of wonder, past lavender and lilies, past even flowers of gold, through the field. Then it opens to display the sound I've been hearing...

A river so brilliant with a greenish blue hue, yet crystal clear and pure! Sun danced, with multi-prismatic shafts of living color dancing upon it! As outstanding as this living water is, the source of each droplet's life is standing upon it. Jesus, full of radiant wonder is there! I watch for a moment – captivated – for the light of the glorious beauty of His being is stunning! He glances at me and smiles. His smile is inviting and captivating. Every sunrise and every flame, every torch and every name dances from the depths of Jesus' gaze. I'm held in awe. I watch as dripping glory from His eternal love, droplets of pure light touch the water and cause it to come alive. Each orb is like a clear raindrop, covered in color and set ablaze with a mini flame that reflects and refracts everything around it in droplets of liquid rainbow fire. As Jesus' glory drips onto the living waters a sort of "steam essence" comes up; a humidified atmosphere of life, pure life. "Come." He beckons without words. "Come." I do. Before I enter His River of Life, the very atmosphere of liquid glory-steam enters me. The glory of Jesus' being touches the stream and lets off a permeating mist, a sizzle, as water and His glory fire unite to create living air. I inhale His mist. Every particle of living breath enters me. I am at once so alive and yet so still. Inside the fiber of my cells the atoms of my being unite in a glorious response to breath and weightlessness. Peace fully enters me; living fire-water, glory steam, stillness, complete stillness... He leads me beside the still waters. Now I am one with stillness.

He catches my gaze and I am satiated with the fire of His stare. Still. I belong to Him. I am one in, on and through His mist of life. I return His stare. Each holy beam of His brilliant stare penetrates past layers of humanity. Beams like hot oil, but soothing, calming and comforting all thoughts besides Him. Remember Me. Remember Me, and every tender moment, every loving thought, every bit of goodness in every touch surfaces in me. I am free as the heat of His stare quiets my soul. In this holy bright fire, in the penetrating awakening of pure burning desire, I know nothing is impossible.

Instead of questions there is peace. Instead of thoughts there is love.

In the center of my spirit I marvel at His most precious flow. He smiles so brilliantly. He takes my hand and smiles again. Then, slowly, He places his left hand behind my neck and lowers me down until I am immersed. As my body surrenders under the water my eyes stay locked on His. My face goes completely under. I gasp for a second thinking, "I'll drown!" Yet, as I gasp the rivers flow, glory fire enters my lungs, surrounds my heart's valves and takes over. Beyond self-preservation's death, His flow now overrides all function. There is no thought to breathing. I am one with eternal breath, alive, beyond life – eternal. I needn't even breathe for under His living flow I know, as I am known.

Be still and know that I am God.

He leads me besides (inside) the still waters. His river is full and so am I. Water like jewels surrounds me. He brings me up as heavenly angels appear. They appear to witness the baptizing of my being into what I was created to be, an expression and image of His glory. I return now Jesus' stare of pure life. Full of Him, I return His love in me, upon Him again. I am grateful, thankful, yet content to just be. The angels form a winged canopy. Jesus brings me unto His chest. Never have I known a love like this. "Be, Still, Breathe." "I will never ever leave, just be and breathe Me."

2

HEART TORN APART

So, one may ask me at this point, "If you've had these encounters, why aren't you okay?" I didn't know at the time that these living exchanges were my 'safe place', and I separated every good and loving thing out from me, including my very heart's beat, lest anyone take it, beat it, or rape it out of me again. It's like I put it on a shelf of safety, my hiding place, and I only told a few of my experience. As they laughed and mocked Him I learned to keep the details secret... Yet again, a house divided against itself cannot stand. Nor a mind, fragmented in pain. And now, the physical pain from the car accident prevents me from "escaping", and is pulling me apart. As my body betrays me in this place of love, I'm wiped out. Pain jerks my emotions and grounds my heart as it demands a response. The physical aches from a fractured spine, jammed body, and crammed legs demand immediate action. I am screaming inside out, "Answer me! Answer my plea of pain! Where did You put Your pain God?" He reveals that the physical pain I am feeling right then began a long time ago. He invites me again to come, come away, into the valley of the shadow of death, full of memories, painful yet true. "Let me show you Cathy, what happened to you."

At the age of two I had Rheumatic Fever. It is an extremely dangerous fever that can affect the heart, and ultimately, the life of a child. This was over fifty years ago. My mother would check my temperature, watch for spikes and call the doctor immediately when it was high. During the night I often would get hot. Every minute counted and so my mother would draw an ice-cold bath, (remember I'm only about two) and place me in it until the doctor could be reached. Inside the tub were many cold washcloths. These washcloths were placed on my back over and over again. Just as they got warm from the heat off my back, they would be replaced. Another cloth, another cold touch, another cold bath, when all I wanted was to be warm, to be held and warm. The very source of this warmth, my mother, was placing those washcloths on my back in this tub, this cold, cold place. – Cry? She said I rarely did. Warmth did not come and somewhere deep inside I learned it does no good to cry, to feel, it will only be met by a cold washcloth. I had no idea that I had already learned this, as another had already touched me and taken all my trust and innocence away. No one could hold me then, either. But I mustn't cry, I mustn't feel, or something worse than cold will happen.... Suddenly, a deep horror came back in a dream. It, the molestation, was shown to me like this:

"I mustn't cry. I mustn't feel or something worse than 'cold' will happen

---

And there "she" was, me at around 2 or 3; brilliant, boisterous, beautiful. I'm standing at a wall writing "ABC" and "Jesus loves me." Why? How can she know that? Jesus loves her? Hah! Yet even at this very tender, innocent toddler age, my blue eyes told another story. Without warning a huge club comes from behind her and smashes her head in. Blood and brains smatter upon the wall. Who would do this to this baby? Lust and Seduction is their name. Having possessed an innocent, weak human, their goal is to destroy all innocence and purity. Molestation claimed its prize, and as a baby, something inside dies. Yet, let's hide this baby so no one can find out she knows His name. With a head wound that causes fear of existing, that innocent part of me disappears into safety. The sickness that my perpetrator took out on me, became a cloak and dagger of fragments and fractures in the mind on its way to becoming a multiple. Little girl is lost, at oh such a high cost. Tears of fear flow out of my eyes, comfort denied, the separation begins.

Sickness entered my mind that day, the day of molestation, accompanied by pain and suffering. A high fever is the first to show its form and I am held carefully for what seems the first time. Hmmm... Pain and suffering get me held, comforted, and medicated. Even at two years old the wrong connection has begun. Comfort and pain, pain and comfort – hmmm.... Though never

fully conceived, the seed of pain and suffering is implanted. This caused a split in my brain that "lied" against the picture language in my heart, His garden of love. They, the eyes of my heart, were never smashed (BBE, Ephesians 1:18). So as a gift, I could always see the soundness in Him, it's just that my mind could not convey that heart sight. Jesus is the only way, so the eyes of my heart stayed with Him as my mind turned away from the horror it could not carry. My mind talks to me and says, "Go away little girl, pretend it's okay. Come away to a much safer place." I did go away inside myself. My heart was placed by my mind into: "Jesus loves me, this I know, for the Bible tells me so. Little ones to Him belong. They are weak but He is strong." My mind continues, "Keep this little girl in this place to protect her from cold, cold touch." "We are broken," my mind continues, "so we, apart from little girl, must be unlovable. So we must try to be good; so, so good. Then we won't be placed in the cold."

There came a true separation inside of me that I am consciously unaware of. Fragments and pieces, devoid of original feelings form in my mind; just safety "rooms". Anger here, sickness there. But love? Oh, not love. Only the purest place in Jesus' world can take me there. That place, innocence and love, was protected by other rooms inside of me, denial, fear, pain, addiction, anything that would keep the inner child safe from harm again. Many years of mastering fake feelings followed. I would watch hours of emotional movies to study people's reactions and copy them in any given instance, watching responses so as to memorize reactions to pacify people. I must get this right. Then they would leave me alone.

The seed of pain hid itself for many years. I was on medication for having a heart murmur and so I was "special". "Don't upset her, don't run too fast, and don't do too much, because Cathy is the sickly one." Not much more happened until I was fifteen. I always knew Jesus and went to church. I got totally involved in the Jesus movement and was somewhat carefree. There was always something missing, but because I had to take pills for my heart to be strong, no one gave me a second thought. No one realized I was silently delayed because of molestation's toll that day. But oh how my mind could fake living until a horrible accident one day.

3

BRAIN PAIN

Being carefree and fifteen, I hopped into my friend's car, off to burgers and fun. Somewhere along the way (all of this I had to be told) a car smashes into us; into the passenger's side where I was sitting. (I was told if I was wearing a seat belt that day, I would be dead.) The impact of the other vehicle ramming into me, threw my body into the dash board as my face smashed against the radio. Immediately the left orbital bone floor of my eye, and my nose were smashed and broken.

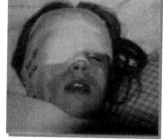

It seems ironic that the key features of the human brain that allow us to design and drive automobiles are also our greatest liability in the event of a crash. With its massive size and high organization, the human brain can literally pull itself apart under the physical forces associated with traumatic brain injury. In particular, axons in the

white matter appear poorly prepared to withstand damage from rapid mechanical deformation of the brain during trauma. In contrast, diffuse brain injury may occur in the absence of impact forces but is dependent on inertial forces that are commonly produced by motor vehicle crashes, and in some cases, falls and assaults.[1]

Fig. 2. An idealized representation demonstrating diffuse brain injury resulting from an inertial force. Rapid rotational acceleration/deceleration of the head in the coronal plane (yellow arrow) results in the deformation of the entire brain. The falx membrane along the sagittal midline acts as a barrier to lateral brain motion (blue arrow), creating high strain between the hemispheres. This overall mechanical deformation results in diffuse axonal injury with prominent axonal pathology in midline structures.

What remained undiagnosed was my brain was thrown against the inside of my skull as the fragments of eye flooring and nose chips broke away. I had an accident in my brain; therefore I was never the same. Technically a DAI, Diffused Axonal Injury, occurs when a brain is smashed against the inside of one's skull. It causes many things like: death, being brain dead, poor impulse

---

"A simple question of "How are you?" triggered at least five different responses in me at one time, thereby short circuiting any answer."

---

control, and inability to process information and reason. It is called 'diffused' because after the original injury, it continues to spread. As the brain heals, it scars over places where neuron pathways are interrupted. Once information is received in the brain, the process for filing and responding to outside information can be permanently altered. Yet forty years ago there was not an emphasis on brain injuries. Therefore my body eventually

healed, yet I was on my way to being every name in the book; ADD, bipolar, and sociopath.

Little did they know; little did I know! I was called mentally challenged, stubborn, stupid and rebellious. When the pain in the brain got so bad, Jesus would come. I would switch off my brain and go to the heart place for hours on end. Questions that people and/or counselors would ask of me, I could not answer. I never knew why. I only knew I would try and the signals never stayed the same in my brain. A simple question of "How are you?" triggered at least five different responses in me at one time, thereby short circuiting any answer. The answers were all there, "I'm fine. Why do you want to know? The last person that asked me that used it against me. If I don't answer correctly will you punish me?"

Imagine all these responses coming in one instance to a simple question? My brain actually overloaded and I would get this blank stare on my face. I couldn't even answer with the response of "I don't know" because I did know. I just couldn't retrieve the answer in a singular fashion. Hence, stalemate, more medication and another label – "Special, oh, she's special." Right! If they would just stop asking me questions, I would be anything they wanted me to be. Just leave me alone, so I can go away.

I truly knew Jesus. I was greatly gifted and anointed. I could give meanings of the Bible that would puzzle most. I would prophesy and intently pray. Yet, as soon as I was out of this "safe" church setting I would change. Again, I didn't know. I would be dumb, not making much sense in certain areas, and if I were asked about something I prophetically spoke in church, fear walls would immobilize my words and I would go blank. I was therefore "odd", "not all there". I had no idea. I did, however, know something was wrong, for I always seemed a step behind in catching the hang of life – except for Christ, my safety. But on the outside I could lie, steal, and stab you in the back with nary a thought. Stealing became a "high"; a way to get back at all the "whosoevers" in life.

This, of course, conflicted with the true heart of love that had been buried somewhere inside. The more I stole, the more I lied. I would show "them". As I would get caught I learned to run away, far away. "I didn't steal." I would think deep inside, "You just didn't hear my cry." Faced with rapes, drugs and a child out of control, my mother and dad would plead with me all they could. "Just don't leave," Mom would plead, and I'd say, "Okay," truly meaning it, and be gone in a few hours, running from pain, running from feeling anything again. Suicide attempts, drugs and wild times became my norm. I had no impulse control.

I was out of control and they did what they had to do for a fourteen/fifteen year old. They put me in a hospital (not just a hospital, but a sanitarium/mental hospital) for three months, not knowing where they had left me, I froze and was unmanageable. My mother and father pleaded, "Just help her please. She's hurting herself and we can't help her."

4

SANITARIUM

I had been in juvenile jail several times. I had been warned and counseled. But this? This was new. In a fit of absolute fear and rage, I hear someone screaming. It's me. I am taken to a bed, strapped in with restraints, and drugged. Wow! A consequence beyond my control! And as horrible as it may have seemed to be "put away", it wasn't half as horrible as not knowing why I was in there. Most of my brothers and sisters, my parents would go to therapy sessions for me. I would be asked questions on how I felt about this or that. I did not have an answer, really.

Everything inside was numb, empty and "safe". My one sister, I remember, cried, asking, "Why does she just stare like that?" Then, turning to me, she'd say, "Just answer Cathy. What did you feel when you were placed here?" "I felt nothing." Yet inside I am thinking, "What behavior can I copy so I can leave this place." There are no previously learned reactions to practice here, so when left alone, all parts of feelings come rushing in at once. Hence, screaming fear and manic fits, feelings suppressed in fear, make their appearance outside of my control.

Am I aware of this then? Oh, no! This understanding took years of integrating into Christ Jesus, in the base of love that would never leave. This is why so much repetition had to happen in me. Each level of thought needed a record of its own to finally be united into one source: God. God is love.

5

HIDE IT DEEP

So with A.D.D., a "new" disease, Mom was given a prescription and I was soon (three months) released. In all of this I had to "give in", be good and study hard. It will be okay; otherwise they will put me away. To me, Jesus Christ was the only real person. For everyone else, I played the "game". I was better, sweeter, yet deep inside I cried out to Him, to Jesus, to make me understand. He would always answer me. Jeremiah the prophet is imploring the Lord for an answer also. It reads: "Why is my pain perpetual and my wound incurable, refusing to be healed? Will You indeed be to me like a deceitful brook, like waters that fail and are uncertain?" God answers Jeremiah in the next verses, "...If you return [and give up this mistaken tone of distrust and despair], then I again will give you again a settled place of quiet and safety, and you will be My mouthpiece; and if you separate the precious from the vile [cleansing your own heart from unworthy and unwarranted suspicious concerning God's faithfulness], you shall be My mouthpiece. [But do not yield to them.] Let them return to you – not you to [the people]. And I

will make you to this people a fortified, bronze wall; they will fight against you, but they will not prevail over you, for I am with you to save and deliver you out of the hands of the wicked, and I will redeem you out of the palms of the terrible and ruthless tyrants."

(A.M.P., Jeremiah 15:18-21)

The Living Bible states it like so: "Why do I keep on suffering? Why are my wounds incurable? Why won't they heal? Do You intend to disappoint me like a stream that goes dry in the summer?" To this the Lord replies, "If you trust Me I will show you, and you will be My mouthpiece again. Instead of talking nonsense, you will proclaim a

worthwhile message. You will be My love letter. The people will trust you and you will not need to defend yourself to them. I will make you like a solid bronze wall. They will fight against you, but will not defeat you. I will be with you to protect and keep you safe. I will rescue you from the power of wicked and violent people. I, the Lord, have spoken." (Living Translation, Jeremiah 15:18-21)

To me at this time, the "wicked people" and ruthless tyrants were fragments inside my own psyche. Do not turn to "them". I listened to nothing but the Word of God that said HE would give me a place of settled quiet. He would protect me. He would defend me against my own self, even to the point of being impenetrable (a fortified bronze wall) in my heart to anything but Him. In the Word it says: "If your eye is single your whole body is sound." (KJV, Matthew 6:22) So I set out to pursue even more of Him. He is all I knew, anyway.

6

STILL BE

How do I separate the precious from the vile in my own being? How? I am so tired of what I don't know. Pieces of memory will flash for a moment, only to be swallowed up again, somewhere. I don't even know my own being? Your love is spilling over into me. Now what? How can my mind and heart unite as one? Isaiah says, "The heart of the rash will understand knowledge, and the tongue of the stammerers speak plainly." (KJV, Isaiah 32:4) Perhaps then, there is hope. How do I bring a heart into its home; into me?

It is a vision encounter that brought my heart of broken love into the fullness of Jesus. Touch had become pain. Touch and pain. I can't have one without the other. They must go together. So finally, tired and worn, the Lord shows me myself as an adult, carrying what seems to be a little child. But, the child, me, is very, very limp. What follows in these next few paragraphs is how God integrated my inner child into the adult. This will not be written "properly", however it is written as an adult whose inner child is dying. My inner love, my child trust, was dying inside. I am an adult in places and bring her, the child, to Him in pleas and passion. "I" also answer as adult, child. To identify who is speaking at what time, to me, is to destroy the pure plea... so bear with me...vision:

Adult Cathy is carrying innocent love Cathy in her arms. As I carry her to Him, I am exhausted and deeply afraid of her. She is everything sweet. She is pretty, but not at this moment. She is everything that has been beaten and raped out of me, the grown up Cathy, and I wish to stop her, to somehow stop her. "You are too trusting and loving; so stupid to feel. Come along with what I know. This way you will not get hurt. Get away. Get away." But baby Cathy never left; never left the only One she knew. She never left, dear God, You. "Come on," Adult says, "Let's numb it then it will go away. Let's run so fast no one will know your name. No one can stop you to find out who you are, for love and innocence have no part in me."

The mind of the adult steps in and addresses the child's heart, "You know better, you were so told." So, wearing that "jacket" of "Why, yes, yes I do!" hardened me as intelligence rationalized and separated me from love. Knowledge apart from love covered all the questioning when I got older. Cover up and flee! Pastor, Evangelist and Nursing degrees are trying to bury the purity. Yet, deep down inside of me Little Girl loved, played, hoped, screamed, and bled. "Not love," Adult chimes in, "You'll see. Grow up now." Yet I, as His loving child, continued to believe that love would not die inside; inside our secret place.

Time takes its toll as Adult loses love and hope, having covered it over with drugs, knowledge and escapism. Death begins as Addiction's cry wracks Adult's body. Frightened because she can't even hear her Child's cry in her heart any more, Adult pleads now with God as Loving Child is limp in Adult's arms. "How long will it go on? Can you help her? She's almost gone; gone by words of shame, dismissal and pain. Words as weapons were slicing and cutting. Blades of brutality are beating love into pain and I am so afraid. Love is pain."

Adult surrounded herself with knowing it all, every situation. What's the possible outcome? If it were a church setting, who's preaching? What are they about? If it's at home, what are Mom and dad doing? What mood are they in? Adjust. Pick a face. Put it in place. Adjust quickly, life and death. No hidden slaps of words sharper than ice picks, much less chance of getting noticed! Catch the clues fast to keep the image strong. "I'm okay. You're okay".

Yet, where did I go wrong? I'm dying and I don't know why. Quietly God's whisper comforts me, "Be still." Although Adult had sought Him, His direct kindness frightens her again! Adult runs faster, harder, longer to stop Love's whisper. He's talking much too loud now. Get behind the cloud of familiar smiles, such style, as blood and dirt cake down Child's face. It's almost too late to just make it stop for a moment, to stop hurting. Get away. Go away, finally away, and permanently. "Just take this bottle of pills. It will never hurt again. No more feeling. No more touch. There, there now..."

God's/Love's whisper to be still, roars louder and stronger. "Be still, be still." And yet still the pain knew her, contorted her, was her. Adult is now terrified and pleads again on Child's behalf, "Can you help me, help her?" Limp and ragged, small and nearly breathless, Adult Cathy finally holds Love Cathy up to Whisper in a desperate plea, "Please don't touch her, umm... me. I hurt so deeply, Father God." Whisper smiles at me. "I will not touch you, yet I will uphold you with My Word."

God brings me more understanding about the end of that encounter and I will explain more. The stillness it produced, however, carried on. The right to live! I had already tried to commit suicide. Now to enter the love of Christ who had already died, gave me such a reason to be alive still (still). Then He carries on. Father God breathes on Adult as she holds Child and 'both' float gently into the cradle of His arms. His breath, His whisper, His Word protects her flesh from even His touch like a force field; a shield. Child Cathy responds and finds His gaze. Adult must look, too, for 'both' are in one place. "Look at me. Keep my tender eyes as your focus." We do, and Father releases many angels to rub oil and salve into her unfeeling body. "Shhh...Shhh...Shhh..." Father loves me this I know. And touch begins to be released from frozen horrors as the angels apply balms of glory's depth. Touch is awakened.

Whisper then responds again, "Shhh, be still. Be... Still... Still... Be, Be, Still be, Still, Be." And slowly I, Adult, realize that it mattered to

Him. All the while He knew that she/I would try to die quietly. He had sent His Word before her/me, to save me. Be still, still be – the right to exist, the right to be alive, the right to live. To be, to be! Still! I see Jesus on the cross. And when pain was hung, crucified, He opened up His only Son so that I saw a room in His side. I walk up to His side with the separated pieces of my heart in my arms. By the time I get to Christ, I'm small enough to "go in". I turn myself around so my back is touching Jesus' pierced side, still carrying my heart in my arms, and I back into Him, the womb of the Morning Star. Into the One who had already died. I go into His side, the open side of Him who had already died. In His pierced, torn, bloodied flesh, it had been done. I back into the chest of God's own Son. Into His side, His spear-pierced side, with Child on my lap. I'm alive, and every vein that ever flowed, covered in the blood of Whisper's Son's pain, all pieces of separation become one again, lying in the whole, "hole" in Him. Inside.

I back into His side until I touch up against His spine and I sit. I lean my head against His bones, tilt my head upward and sigh. Home, I'm home in Christ. As I hold onto my feeling, Child, now in my lap, resting my head upon His spine, I see Christ's broken, pierced heart. Slowly, blood and water trickle upon my brow, my head, my eyes, my cheeks, and permeates my being. Rest, Oh Lord, rest is dripping! Love's quiet strength is flowing, knowing; knowing as His life's flow warms and washes away all the unknown. It doesn't matter here.

Warmth flows, not on but through, penetrating past all my defenses. My head doesn't hurt anymore. How long has it been since my head didn't hurt? Hurt. Past hurt; when my brains were smashed against the wall as my innocence and heart were stolen by another's will. My head, I'm not hurt, my brains, not shattered, Your warmth, Your flow, Your head...Your head!? Your head took my blow. You took my blow of innocence lost as the thorns pierced purity's price for me. You were pure innocence as You went to the cross, for me, for my head, and my heart. Once and for all I am suddenly yet sweetly aware that the inner heart, Love Child Cathy whom I hold in my lap, needs to come home, home in Adult me.

The very blood spilled from Your heart onto my head purposely goes past my neck, removing all stiff-necked attitudes, past my shoulders, no longer heavily laden, these both lifted by Your price, Your sacrifice. I sleep.

Your blood continues, now flowing past ribs and fortresses too many to name. They can't stand against Your love's flow, anyway. Now, onto my inner child resting on my lap: Your blood and power beckon my heart's response. "Now Cathy, open your heart to take her in just as you've done it for Me." I know I can. I know I should. Yet, just one question I plead, "I am an adult and if I take her in, what if she disappears? I am an adult and Your blood is the heart of One, in everything. Yet, what if I hurt Child Cathy, like the others who were grown? What if it gets so bad like before and I just 'throw her out' cause it hurts so much to feel? Oh Lord, what if...I miscarry her too?" What? I never miscarried, yet suddenly, in the shelter of Jesus' pierced side; I am thrust into a memory, hidden internally.

I am nearly sixteen, on the run again from home, heading towards the apartment of a boyfriend that had just dumped me. I started down the single flight of stairs. Suddenly, I am violently overcome by wracking cramps and unbearable pain. All I remember next is a huge pool of blood at my feet, my legs are soaked from top to bottom, and all I know is there is a mess and I made it. I will be in so much trouble for making a mess I ran as fast as I could behind a gas station where I had a sleeping bag between two trash cans. Please God, don't let them catch me, I didn't mean it. I will not do it again, oh God help me. I fell into a fitful sleep, changed clothes and showered in the gas station's sink...and neatly blocked out the miscarriage for fear of being found in a weakened condition...Oh Lord. Father God answers, "My blood, My Son's blood is love, for I loved you so much I gave Him for you, that as you believe Cathy, you, your true you, kind, loving, feeling, whole, kind Cathy would not die. Not die, but have eternal life, eternal, and forever.

So, will all of your children. Your other child is with Me. Let's get child Cathy home first. Just believe.

I am satisfied yet ask one more thing. "May I write a poem from her about how she knows You?" Father agrees, and so totally embracing Love; Child Cathy gives her testimony: She sees Jesus on the cross.

My Jesus, I'm not even three
but even I know you're not supposed to be in a tree.
You could get hurt.
So can you come down and play?
The way we did yesterday?
I see your scratch; the one on Your feet.
I'll get flowers and kiss it to make it better.
See?
For You shouldn't be in a tree,
You could get hurt

Father's tears join His Son's blood and water as I then look at Him. It's time, I'm ready. As the blood and water flow on and though me I hear the song I've never forgotten. "Jesus loves me, this I know." My adult knows this song! "For the Bible tells me so. Little ones to Him belong", my inner child! "They are weak but He is strong! Yes, Jesus loves me," now just one voice, "Yes, Jesus loves me," one heart, one voice, one love. Adult and inner child are one, "for the Bible tells me so." I relish in the blessing of unity.

Father draws attention to something, someone in His arms. It is a soft small bundle of; why it's a baby! And yet somehow I know her. Father God smiles, and says "At 16 you thought you miscarried a baby. Yet I carried her to me and have kept her for you till you would remember. You will never fear miscarrying life again, either in your womb, your mind, or your heart here. This is who you lost, Cathy. I've kept her for you. This is your child, safe with me." The baby in His arms is singing, "Jesus loves Me," and glances at me. Never have I seen a love like this. So pure, so strong, so... "She's a part of you in Me, Cathy. I've held her for you. Do you want to name her?"

Now, here I am, in the side of Christ, fully one in Him for less than thirty seconds, yet I respond with the most amazing protective, full-fledged, no-holds-barred love — for another! My child, she hadn't been "miscarried", no! For Father God carried her for me, to love. To love as a whole person and the first encounter besides Christ is my child. I wept so purely with joy. Oh child, you are so, so beautiful. You are my little girl, my little, little girl. Oh Lord, she's perfect! Then He smiles at me, in His Son's side, unified, and says, "So are you." I see His face, His adoration His smile, and I am captivated. "How do I love thee? Let me count the ways..."

I start with this! "Through the love of Your Son, now in me. I kiss Your face, Father. I kiss and pat Your cheek. I love You, Father. Teach me to love You as You have loved me, wholly, whole heartedly." Father replies, "It is finished." Finished... and I am no longer in Jesus. He is in me. He is in me! One in Him! My heart and His are one. I am home!

"The Word of God is quick and powerful and sharper than any two-edged sword, piercing even to the dividing asunder of soul and spirit, and of the joints and marrow, and is a discerner of the thoughts and intents of the heart." (KJV, Hebrews 1:14) I am in the Word of God. The world separated my "self", inner being, from the core of my inside. However, the Word of God, which, since "...God is love..." (KJV, 1 John 4:8), the very sword that I would think would separate me has now become the sword that separates the darkness out of my identity as fully loved in Him. God's word separated me from the lie that I had miscarried. God's word separated out from the core of my being that I would hurt my inner child. He separated dark perception, hell, and in so doing I'm in His side, separated unto Him, and that which separated me from myself in the world, pain, rape, etc., now bows to the higher law – God's Son being separated from His Father in order that He would come and join me to and in Him forever!

"In the beginning was the Word, the Word was with God, and the Word was God." (KJV, John 1:1) As I am in the Word, God, I'm also in the beginning, in God, as He said, "And the earth was without form, and void. He said, "Let there be light, and my void, all that was separated from Him came into being in me as I sat in His heart, one with Him, in Him, through Him, by Him – one, undivided. "For I am persuaded that neither death, nor life, nor angels, nor principalities, nor powers, nor things present, nor things to come, nor height, nor depth, nor any other created thing, shall be able to separate me from the love of God that is in Christ Jesus my Lord." (KJV, Romans 8:38-39 [emphasis "mine"])

"For as many as are led by the Spirit of God, they are the sons of God. For ye have not received the spirit of bondage again to fear; but ye have received the Spirit of adoption, whereby we cry Abba, (Daddy) Father." (KJV, Romans 8:14-15)

7

ABBA BLAZE

Pain, the pain of separating feelings from reality, has begun. Each time God would come, each time He walked with me and talked with me through His living and written Word, I was able to believe deeper and deeper. In Isaiah it says, "The heart also of the rash shall understand knowledge, and the tongue of the stammerers shall be ready to speak plainly." (KJV, Isaiah 32:4) The heart of the rash?! (Strong's H4116) Rash: Driven, fast, hurried. The heart?! (Strong's H3824) Heart: Inner man, mind, will, heart, soul, understanding, midst. Shall I go on? I must! Strong's continues the definition as: thinking, reflection, memory, inclination, resolution, determination of will, conscience, seat of appetites, emotions and passions, as a seat of courage! What? My heart that used to be rash... my heart, which encompasses all the definitions I just wrote... My Heart shall understand knowledge! Now my heart in Him – in me – can understand! In the (Strong's H995) Understand: To feel, attend, perceive, discern. Knowledge means: Aware, wisdom, perception (Strong's H1847). So, in all of this I can feel again, be loved, perceive fun, joy, peace. I can laugh without guilt!

Oh, I truly have it made, as if all that ever happened was for this; walking and talking and integrating other levels of separation into You Lord. You are my friend! My buddy! How much fun we are finally having, making up for lost time! Ahhh, Yes! The pain of having feelings, or not having feelings was truly done, and God was very patient and kind as I enjoyed this friendly love. Yet, pain has many levels, and Father God, (who no longer had to whisper) needed me to perceive and be aware of the depth of His love, not just friendship. He brought me into another level, a depth past the necessary childlike joy, past carefree days. The stage of a heart that is separated from its Creator, from God, is the most severe, and Father God needed me to know another deeper level of the price of this love, His love.

"Truly, I didn't do in on purpose, I was just so self-focused for Him that I never thought about anyone else. I had a voice and I intended to use it."

Now my child heart, who knew Jesus but had been silenced for so long, found a voice – His voice, His Word, Him, Him, Him. I talked and talked and talked about where I'd been, what He'd done, to anyone at any time. I knew something for "real" and wasn't going to be quiet. I didn't care, in a way, about other people. I had the answer. I knew more than them. I could see, and He loved me "so I'll help you to see too." I, at this point, was a spoiled child with a living flame that burnt instead of kindled other fires in His name. Not ever being considered for having much of anything to offer, I was now a child with a "new found toy" – Jesus. If you seemed technically or academically smarter than me I'd just whip out a vision and tag it on to your last comment. Truly, I didn't do in on purpose, I was just so self-focused for Him that I never thought about anyone else. I had a voice and I intended to use it. The trouble would come when the depth of the visions and encounters never caused me to think on anyone else for very long. "What did I see? What did he tell me? Let me tell you!" Oh, the visions and encounters are real. I just never got any deeper other than my child heart, which had found its home, in Him.

But, a child with a flame is not for burning people. In fact, my flesh was still creeping with all kinds of actions. When one of my former friends would pray for the new believers I would act out. If they needed prayer for sickness, I'd get sick. For deliverance from abuse, I'd be abusive. Soon this friend and Pastor said, "Cathy, I don't know what's wrong with you but you have to go. Your words from God are so true and pure, yet I don't understand why you act out every time there is prayer." I was sent by her to a beautiful camp for inner city children. She knew I could pray for them for hours in my room where I would not interact with them. She said, "Ask God, Cathy, to show you what's wrong. Why is this attitude about Jesus so deep set, yet your actions speak another language?"

Now, I had been with this woman for many years so I trusted her insight. I went up to a place in the Sequoias. I searched for God's answer with tears and shame. "If what I was doing caused more harm to You, help me to know Your holy name." I was truly hurting more people than I knew and I was more afraid of my future than I was of my past.

DR. CATHLEEN M. SCHMITT

8

IN LOVE

As I wept in the middle of the woods, I went into a vision with the Lord. Parts of it went like this: Jesus again is walking with me. We are on a beach, which is our most favorite place to meet, besides the garden, that is. Always, when I saw Him, we have this greeting: He would smile and I always put His hair behind His ear so I could better see His face. This day started no different, yet something was different. I just didn't know what.

We walk past the beach and a garden of delight. Everything seems all right. He motions me to sit on a hill right next to Him. I, of course, just want to see what He will show me that day. Would it be rainbows with fiery wings? Butterflies with lion heads? What's next? What now?

He smiles, looks directly at me and says, "I love you. Full on. I love you." Now, Child Cathy who's been having a ball in an adult heart has been in control. Yet, this look, this stare, this profession from Christ was not to the childlikeness in my heart. It was to the whole. "Adult in charge – I love you."

Instantly all the old "guardians" of Child Cathy pop up to put their two cents in. Denial is first, "Oh, surely not I!" Fear chimes in,

"Run!! Hide!" Yet, actually, everything just kind of goes numb inside. Condemnation, Control and Guilt chime in, "We've done pretty good without You. You have the kid so leave us alone." All I could do is stare. I, as an adult, have no response to love, especially to love spoken so purely and directly and complete. "But You're my friend, Jesus. The walks, the laughter, You never mentioned love to me. I just don't know. I don't want to know. I just want a friend."

Jesus smiles again and again states, "I love you." His voice is so strong and true. The intent of His words slice like a sword through my being. I am struck dumb, yet scream without speech, "No!" My eyes bulge white with fear. "No, please. Please, not love." "I love you," He replies, quiet as His Father's Whisper tone, yet pounding me as a full-blown storm. My heart implores Him to stop! "Don't You know?! Don't You See?! Please, turn Your eyes from me! I hurt the ones I love. I am truly, unlovable."

"I love you," Jesus Christ replies, this time spoken with passionate urgency. I respond, driven by a survival terror deep within me. I strike His face hoping to silence this torture!

"I love you," came the sure reply; never blinking, somehow softer yet stronger than before, as I bruise His face. "I love you," His only reply, as myself, my very self, strikes with the very words spoken by abuses gone by. Locked away behind doors of a child, as stolen innocence and trust not even allowed its full birth, prematurely abducted as another took their will out on her; locked away behind rape, behind cursing, behind outright lies. Physical or mental mattered not as the blows of "love" – angry love, drove love into being quiet. It will all pass, all in the name of this love. Love is pain. Pain is love. No, thank you. As He continues to speak those words I am overcome with fear, trying to silence the very mouths of others who had professed the same thing.

I beat and strike at this word, this "love." Blacking out in a furious beating frenzy until something wet is on my hands, bringing me somewhat to my senses. I stop cold. It's blood! Blood? Whose blood is on my hands? Whose blood is on my hands?!

I hear a barely audible groan and am forced to stop the horrible introspection. I glance towards the sound, lifting my head up and I observe Jesus hanging on the cross, whispering in swollen, bruised agony, His gaze heavenward. "Father, forgive her, she knows not what she does." He locks His eyes upon me once more and says in a voice laced with pain, "I Love You." It is finished, and He dies.

I'm stunned, immobilized, as I lower my head to observe the blood on my hands. I look up again so slowly and realize that His death, Christ's death only magnifies His eternal cry of "I Love You!" For what greater love hath a man than He lay down his life for another. Truth: This love, His love, would never, could never be hit away, driven away, yelled, kicked, dismissed or murdered. His love would never, could never leave me nor forsake me. I can do nothing to stop Him from loving me. Christ's love never ends. His love for me never ends. Nothing can separate me from the love of God that is in Christ Jesus...nothing!

As the realization of eternal Love hits me I am still between vision and truth, and am aware that I have killed the only one who can love me. A wave of remorse and heart wrenching sobs rack my body as I grasp His cold, pierced feet. "Return to me. Oh, please don't be

dead. I didn't know. I didn't know. I'm so sorry, so very, very sorry." I cry as I crumple at His feet for what I have done. Crucified God's only begotten Son. I cry for Him now, for His pain, for His call, finally thinking of someone other than myself as His blood dries to a hard flaky crust on my hands.

"Forgive me please, forgive me." I bow in remorse to lament the Lover of my soul, my tears soaking His feet as time stands still. I am bent in remorse upon His cold, cold feet. Suddenly, on the top of my head I feel a drop of something, then another, and another. I slowly lift my head to see from where it came. It's from Jesus' side. This blood, now, is not dead. This blood is alive! I feel the great drops of blood permeate my total existence. I'm stunned as I catch His stare; there is no more pain there. The sky has parted above His head. Resurrections beams are streaming down upon His face. His face!

There are no marks on His face. No thorns, no hand print, as I stare He speaks, "I LOVE YOU"...it then dawns on me like the light of day – I can do nothing to stop Him from loving me. I cannot run, scream, or be angry enough to drive His love away. I cannot even kill His love, for, again...what greater love hath a man that he lay down His life for another? Nothing I can do will stop Him from loving me. I respond back to Him with every atom of my being, "AND I LOVE YOU, TOO!" I rush into His arms and am swallowed up in love. Like a huge tree of life, I come. Yet there's more. In Him, I am facing out as He holds me from behind, overshadowing my very body.

The earthly sun expands like a massive meteor. I'm stunned. Obliterating even the tallest Sequoia tree, this blazing expanse is coming towards me. As it hurtles towards me I see this three dimensional, dark cosmic atom/neutron shaped trilogy, engulfed in stunning, white light. They kept going in and out and around each other like a science experiment on energy. This is all surrounded by the blazing great expanse coming towards me.

"This could kill me" was the most terrifying, absolute knowing I had ever felt. Not just kill me, but like wipe-me-off-the-face-of-the-earth kill me! Like never to have existed at all! Ever! This absolute truth terrified me for a moment. Yet, almost at the same time, my next thought of "I'm not afraid" came just as absolute, just as deep, if not somehow deeper. As soon as this thought finished, the neutron – imploding mass inside of it – burst into nuclear bright brilliance within and upon me. I am slammed, pierced, bombarded, invaded all at once with this energy...this massive, imploding, exploding fire! Words are now my enemy as I search to find expressions of total oblivious joy – that which I only thought I knew – now becomes known and thoughts explode within like fireworks displays of love, oh so much love. Totally, finally, yet beginning, up yet in, on yet through, in, in, in the most vehement blaze of an ever increasing crescendo of fire bomb lava. In, out, up, down, no thoughts, no past, no future, just now...now....now majestic miraculous
majesty of absolute passion's power. Oh my God, I am in love...I AM IN GOD!

The forest explodes with billions of winged like holographic mother-of-pearl, clear, yet still visible, wings of a myriad of angels. Love, explosive, bursting, blazing, brilliant-hot love invades me accompanied by thousands of angels in triumph and bliss. Never have I known a love like this. Trembling, alive, aware, I scream, "I love you Jesus! I'm in love, in love, in love with You!" I walk, I'm in love. I cry, I'm in love. I think, it's in love. I dream, it's in love. Liquid fire, blazing beams shoot inside me, coat me, cover me, swallow me. I disappear in the radiant light. I came out of the woods that night... basking in the Tree of Life.

DR. CATHLEEN M. SCHMITT

9

DIFFUSED FIRE

I spend the next three days mesmerized, baptized, and all I know is, if it took me forever, I would speak of His love. I knew no one should go without being loved; no one. I came home and they said I was "mad." It didn't matter anymore. I would still speak. Say what you may, it doesn't go away. The most vehement flame – Yet this time as I spoke of Him I tried to hear where others were lost. I'd cry for joy knowing He'd come, to rapture them as He did me. Words were my enemy. To speak of His fire, well it was only in 2001. But His Word made flesh in me could not go away. In Song of Solomon it says: "...for love is as strong as death...Its flashes are flashes of fire, a most vehement flame [the very flame of the Lord]!" (AMP, Song of Solomon 8: 6) Vehement means: Violent; acting with great force; furious; very forcible; as a vehement wind; a vehement torrent; a vehement fire or heat. (Webster's Dictionary) The very flames of the Lord, in whatever way possible, I imbibe, eat, and drink His flames.

It has been my "swan song" even to this day. No matter who knows me or very long, they will understand the fire of God is love. Some would say "He's a consuming fire" and yes, that's true. But, He doesn't just take away. When the consuming fire met the blood, it became a covenant blaze of love. Let me explain. Almighty God, as a consuming fire, swallowed up His Son for our sins. Judgment was consumed upon Him. Yet, as He was consumed, He sent the Holy Spirit as tongues of fire upon and within every believer at Pentecost. The tongues of fire didn't just dance on their heads. They were diffused through their very souls! Truly! Diffused, spread out, through their very being!

As Father Almighty consumed His Son, Justice, consuming fire, meets the blood. Justice is met. Blaze of love (Holy Spirit) is sent. Son consumed, crucified, died… to send holy, dancing tongues of fire. "For God so loved the world He gave His only begotten Son, that whosoever believes in Him shall not die, but have eternal life." (KJV, John 3: 16) The fire of the most vehement flame is the love of God revealed to our hearts, to us and towards Him, through the Holy Spirit, in Jesus' name: Love. God Is Love. The most vehement, violent, impetuous, and, moving with great intense force and passion Flame... Almighty, Father, Lord and King is His name.

10

REMORSE

So, how do I get from what I just wrote about to a desperate, agonizing cry of "Where did You put Your Pain?" Let me explain. I couldn't be quiet after that day, September 8, 2001. This time not as a child but as an adult. The purity of a child knowing no one should go without knowing His love. So, of course I told them about the sun exploding, and angels, and I'm in love! Sure! That went over well! NOT. Yet all the ridicule did this time was cause me to seek Him more. For me? No. "How, Oh Lord, how do I let them know of Your love?" I ached for those like me, who have never been able to be loved wholly. So, as I was sincerely in His love, the adult and child Cathy, united by Christ within my core being, made a spectacular base for all the other places that had been fragmented out of me. I was truly beginning to own the place my heart called home. Jesus' heart!

As the years passed, fragments of myself come into the home base of love in Jesus. Beatings, rapes, remorse and escape all blend into His heart of love. He would come to me in worship. One such time He brought me into an eye-to-eye, cheek-to-cheek dance with Him. As He captivated my attention, I was swayed into rhythms of glory. Suddenly, He blew across my shoulder. I laughed and asked Him what He did. Oh, there was mockery hiding behind rejection, never mind now. It's gone as You focused on Me. Always blending pieces of myself into Him. The most dramatic thing is there was always the blood of the Lord in all of the integrated places. The dancing swirl had streaks of red stripes and a whirlwind complete union.

Most of the places that He took me were not too hard at first, a dance, hugs, and deep embracing. After building up trust and the pattern, however, I was faced with a piece of myself I did not believe. Now, I had never been guilty of much. It was always excluded away with a sickness of one kind of another. So here in the eyes of my heart I am shown this dirty, tear-stained, ruffled person. She was kneeling before the cross. "That's not part of me!" I vehemently expressed to Him. "She is so dirty." He smiled and asked me to wait and watch. He goes up to her and touches her face, not just any touch, our touch. His hand, flat from her forehead, down her chin, leaving stripes of blood. She lifts her head and radiantly smiles. "Oh, my gosh, that's our greeting Lord! That's our secret, that's… oh, my goodness, that's me!?" His hand upon my face was His seal to me; His demarcation of love.

"He took it all. Just breathe. Just believe and rest in His Price."

Not able to deny this part of myself any longer, I look to Him. He beckoned me forth and places her in front of me. He then places His palm upon both of us. As the trails of blood streak down, they go through her into me and blend her and I, I and I, and back unto Him, into the tear-stained, blood-dripping, crucified place, where I'll become one in Him unto resurrections flow, clean, pure and one. For months I wept and felt guilt and remorse, real remorse for my actions. It was so unbearable at times. Then His bloody face would remind me, He took it all. Just breathe. Just believe and rest in His price. Then my thoughts were no longer internalized. Always looking up, up, up and unto Him. "Focus, and all these things shall be added unto you." I was learning to think of the effect my actions would have on those around me, not just some random trigger pattern of self-absorbed reaction. His face place, now my heart's place, home.

I was asked to go to China to help with mission work. "Wow!" I thought to myself. "You, Lord, really did say it would be this way." "Rest for there are still many trials, yet rest in Me, in My love's true light. Rest in My delight." "So I did, and You came every day, every night. We walked so much. You drew me away. I'd spend hours a day with You, yet never enough time with You. Before my encounter with God in the Sequoias, I was using some drugs occasionally; Tylenol

III   for a toothache or Motrin for another ache. Yet in this time after Your flame, I never had even an aspirin in my system again! You always came through. There is nothing I can do without You, truly."

DR. CATHLEEN M. SCHMITT

11

IDENTIFYING FALSE ANGELS VS. TRUE AMGELS

The angels that worshiped with me in the woods – many came to share with me about You, Lord, and continue to this day. Your eyes, Your walk, Your tastes, and Your desire for me to desire You! I used to think, "I don't need angels, I have Jesus. I might be deceived by a fallen angel. Besides, I'm not supposed to worship them anyway." Yet in Hebrews it says, "Are they not all ministering spirits, sent forth to minister for them who shall be heirs of salvation?" (KJV, Hebrews

1: 14) And when they appeared in the woods with Christ's resurrection glory fire, I knew only they could understand the magnitude of such a thing. Besides, even Jesus talked with, and needed angels to rescue Him throughout the Word. My sister-in-law, Tina, helped me greatly in this area. She would talk about them as normal as possible. I couldn't understand at first but then the revelation was given to me.

I asked the Lord, "How do I tell the difference between a God angel and a fallen one?" He, the Lord, answered me and said, "My true angels always reveal to you something about Me. They have come with brilliance and jewels, oils and spoils. Yet, all the treasures they share and show are to bring you into an understanding of My nature. For instance, I send you an angel with a brilliant, blue jewel. The jewel itself may be truly brilliant in its own light. A fallen angel will seek you to focus on the prize; the jewel, its brightness, its glow, how far it will shine, what it will do, etc. My angel, however, will bring you a jewel then show you what to do. My angel will place the jewel by My face, to illuminate My ever present, absolute loving gaze to you. Or, My angel may take the jewel, place it in My hand to show you how to rule in a particular circumstance. Then, when you get the jewel, its own beauty is okay, yet, compared to how it magnifies Me, it truly is just a bobble indeed!"

So, anyway (and it took time), I now have angels to help reveal to me God's will!

12

ACCIDENT AGAIN?

I was in a terrible accident. I didn't look messed up. The car was totaled and I walked away...sort of... I'm desperate, with crunched vertebrae and spinal cord cyst compression, and thrust into an endless array of pills and pain. I await the authorization codes and surgery dates for the spinal metal and knee replacement. The removal of cysts from my spinal cord and orthoscopic surgeries are buffered by Morphine, Percocet, and too many other drugs to name.

This is the reference

•   Oxycodone (and its infamous extended-release sibling OxyContin) is called 'legal heroin' because it is chemically almost identical, and just as addictive, just as deadly, and just as hard to kick as heroin.

•   Once you've entered the world of oxycodone dependence or addiction, the only way home is through the door marked Oxycodone Withdrawal.

•   Some brave souls do try to go through that door, but less than 5% ever make it all the way; the rest return to their oxy or whatever narcotics they can get.

•   Oxycodone withdrawal is a horrible and painful trip that absolutely no one wants to take, but a trip that everyone knows they have to take if they are ever to regain their lives.

I am emotionally drained as the highs and lows of the drugs enter my system. This roller coaster of doctors, delays and drugs went from one year into two, then two somehow became ten... Ten years, and then the great, grand news, "Mrs. Schmitt, we now have to replace your other knee. It's just not holding up anymore." "No!" I screamed inside. When they replaced my left knee I almost bled out. They had to cinch the blood from flowing so hard and nerves were damaged in the process. Now, I can hardly walk! If it wasn't for the pain pills I wouldn't be able to walk at all! Not another knee! "Oh God! Where did You put Your pain?"

The act of getting up in the morning is usually a no-brainer for most. As my body awoke, I fought through waves of pain, panic, and a mental list of what had to be done that day. Each physical activity, even something as simple as going to the store, had to be a calculated account of the drug's effect. Will the morphine wear off in the vegetable aisle? Can my knees support my back long enough to finish with the meat section? Better take a Percocet just in case they don't and others will find out how weak you really are. Then you'll be no good to anyone.

They will put you away...too much to take care of...too much. I must make my body work at all costs. It mustn't give out or I'll be put away for good. I often got in trouble as my body was racked... my mind on drugs. But, oh, my heart, it had been captured, captivated, and I couldn't help but share, always. No matter how horrible the pain became, He, Jesus, still held my inner flame. "Yes, yes, we know, Cathy, we know you saw Him again, of course, Of course. Now sit down, chill out and we'll get back to you on that and talk." And talk they would. "Pastor Pill Popper! Hah!" "Let's start some classes on addiction," and so on. I would weep for a moment, then He would come and I would be carried through by Jesus; Through to His garden, His arms, His being; through. I thought love was only feeling good. Jesus had to show me that even He learned obedience through the things He suffered. I didn't understand but I could not deny His name. "Though he slay me, yet will I trust in Him: but I will maintain mine own ways before Him." (KJV Job 13:15)

The accident's effect took weeks to unfold, and pain, pain screamed to be silenced any way possible. I had two herniated discs between my upper shoulder blades, a cyst on my spinal cord (which wasn't found until much later), and knees jammed as I had tried to brake the car, which, after multiple orthoscopic surgeries, needed total knee replacement of the left. Ten years, brand new grandbabies and no time to stop, just the endless balancing of pills in order to perform became my life. If I was weak for any length of time, even a day or so, my husband was aggravated, which made everything worse. He would make sure I went for the surgeries and did worry at first, then, after years he was tired of it all and just worn out. Every time I had to have a medicine refilled he would start in. "We don't have the money this time." "Be nice to me or I won't refill it." There was such agony in my soul as I tried to balance pain, pills, impending surgeries, and a control over money for refills. (Now, this is my encounter, if my husband wishes to share his side of the story, he can write a book.) "Why do you stay with him?" was the most asked question. My heart-answer? Because I truly thought it was my fault for being weak.

Eventually, as the drugs would run out all too soon, I would find other people who could "front" me some until I got a refill. I was so desperate that many times I had to use extra money that my husband would have and I would beg him. He always got them. It became so 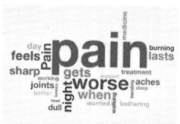 bad towards the end that I would trade, lie, steal drugs from other people's medicine cabinets and not even think twice about what I was doing. Pain was in control and addiction was its twin. Add fear and selfishness and I was a ticking time bomb, a common thief, beggar, liar and cheat. The effect of addiction and pain was an endless self-serving mentality where I became the center of my world. Just get me pills and I'll be good. Just more pills so I can walk, talk, cook, or clean another day. The self-absorbed throne of numbing the pain so as to cope became a vicious cycle, a typhoon of life-sucking terror, just to avoid pain; all pain at all costs.

There is too much pain and I have to keep going. The only true reprieve from this place was my time with the Lord, who would still come to me in my dreams and in my heart to show me in pictures and in His word that He loved me still. And still, with my body ravaged and my mind numb, my heart would still speak to others of Him. He was, and still is, the only true person that never changed and never left me.

The pills, panic and pain overtook my body at my friend's house. The pain of legs that don't work, knees that don't bend, shoulders aching as the metal between the spine crunches, my body bent and my heart so torn it's going to explode. "Your good love is not good enough because I am not good. I'm taking more and more pills to get by. I'm so afraid to feel pain. I'm so afraid to feel. What if I feel and I don't come back? What if I feel to death? I am so angry and tired and frustrated." Ahhh, finally I said it, "Where, Oh where? You are in me and I in You. I cannot be in pain too! Help me to know Your suffering, oh, Father God. Where did You put Your pain when You crucified Your only begotten Son? When it was done?" The pain, I'm screaming inside and out. Quickly the Father opens the door to an amazing scene: "Do you want to see where I put my pain, Cathy?" I'm stunned and yet I answer, "Your pain, where?" It was then that Abba Father, Lord and King opened up His heart for me to see. To see how it was to crucify His Son, not as the Almighty, nor Lord, nor King of kings. What did the Father feel as Daddy? Jesus' Dad, Abba, Father?

13

THE FATHER'S CRUCIFICTION

This is how He showed it to me: Jesus is kneeling in a garden, and as He rises to be betrayed into the enemy's hands, His face is covered with sweat and blood. Abba's bent and brooding focus lends tears of agony with no place to rest. It is, after all, for the best. Judas brings the accusers near and betrayal's breath touches immortal cheek; it is Father's face that recoils in utter disbelief! A kiss? Must it be with a kiss? How betrayal's blade must have shorn into twisted shreds all hope of love. In a kiss, in a Judas kiss, therein lies a weapon sharper than any created. An enemy's lance would have sweetened the blow, for nails pierce only flesh. But this, this kiss bleeds out my heart, my chest. "Oh Father, Father! Take this! Yet not my will but Thy will be done."

His Son's cries shake Father's heart. Not so much for immortal cheek upon which this kiss had landed, but for lips, which He created, that could deliver such a blow. Father's hand reaches to touch His own cheek, to try to wipe off and erase such a sad display. Oh, to touch His own Son's face, one touch. Suddenly, soldiers of crucifixion break the stillness of betrayal's exchange, "Where is He?" With a surge of authority, Jesus replies, "It is I." Taken aback they fall down hard, yet arise for what has begun, the crucifixion of God's only Son.

Now He, who was born to unshackle all, is led away by mere twine. Abba rubs His own wrists, bound by a higher purpose than to loose such mortal chains. Yet, I see Father's face, His face covered with blood and tears, for blows that touched His only Son have assaulted Abba's face as well! Did He feel? What Father would not! Did He feel?! Perhaps not as Almighty or King, yet, Daddy – Dad – was none of these things as His Son's Father. What Father would not, could not, feel and ache as his son must go through death for a higher purpose.

What parent has not had to withhold the very thing their child needs to instill, with assurance, no repeating of wrongs? Yet here Father knows His Son has done nothing except believe that His Father's will is best. Where did You put Your Pain?

Son is beaten unto the bone. Sliced and lashed for those who would be His own. Bloody and ravaged with tendons like strings, muscles wide open in agony.

Father rubs his wrists now, as beating whips and passion's plea, "...O my Father, if this cup may not pass away from me, except I drink it, thy will be done." (KJV, Matthew 26: 42) "Oh Son, Oh Son, Oh Son!" As Father Daddy heaves and sobs, "If only I could, I would."

Piercing brow and splitting flesh, "...Father, forgive them..." (KJV, Luke 23: 34) is all Immortality says. Father stays the swords of millions of Hosts as His back is covered from side to side. Father's hair raises on the back of His neck in wanton disregard of some eternal plan. And just when mortal sword was to take the final blow; as Father, heart in anguish screams, "I...," Bride comes upon the scene, at the beginning, when she/I first saw Father weep, asking, "Father, why are you weeping?" What I didn't know at the time is the answer to Father's cries was that I, as fully resurrected Bride, spoke to His cries, and cared. As the Father turns to look at Bride full of love, full of His eternal love, she draws near to His face and wipes His eyes with her palm. "There Father, there. I'll wipe Your tears. I'll wipe the blood from Your brow. There, there now." Bride comforts Father's anguish as she uses the sleeve of her bridal dress to wipe the spittle off Father's hair. Spittle spewed as He cries out at His Son's distress.

Spit, DNA of man, used to curse the very spit of the Great I Am. Father turns for just a moment, taking in Bride's love of eternal bliss. He catches her captivating gaze in the eternal result of crucifixion's display. One who dared to enter the Holy of Holies of suffering, to freely comfort, with no thought for personal gain, to love Father, not for what He could do but for Love's sake. She holds His face and presses her cheek beneath His massive brow, absorbing the brunt of His pain somehow. His massive head leans gently now towards me. The tears on Father's face were mixed with blood also, as the crown of thorns made their point on the Father's cheek.

There were furrows of deep, unto anguish deep. I draw oil from the fountains of the deep, cradle Your head, and gently pat Your eyes. Tears gently fall from my eyes for Your pain. They fall into Your hair and somehow wash the spittle from accusations lies. Your furrows of blood and pain I meet with oil sweet. A balm gained from redeemed cries from deep unto deep. I apply it with a piece of my bridal cloth from my dress, filling in Your tear and blood-soaked face with eternity's price, now being paid.

I now father you, Father, with that which You have Fathered me. There, there, now, this too shall pass, this too shall pass, You will see. A momentary sigh is released from Father's massive frame. Held now by one who is held in His name. He ponders, to be fathered by His creation for neither goods, nor earthy gain? We exchange a stare, eye to eye, Father and redeemed bride, captive in His eyes. Suddenly eternity is rend, "My God, my God, why hast thou forsaken me?" (KJV, Matthew 27:46). The Holy Father answers true, reflecting to Son what, whom is now captive in His eyes.

Son sees bride in His stare and thus replies;
into Your hand I commit my Spirit,
and dies.

It is finished, it is done.

"Father where did You put Your pain?" Father reaches down near Christ's bleeding side, "Where did You put the pain of addictions' ugly condemning lies? What about the pain of betrayal in my own heart? You come for me all the time, yet in the Judas despair, in the core of my nature, I chose pills over You. I chose my need as You showed me how You bled! What about the pain of shame? The shame of pain, of denying Your name?!" I should have known better. I could have done it, should have seen it. All the "could have, would have and should haves" torment me with the fact that I only love me, but I long to be set free! Yet, I too yelled, "Crucify!" I'm swept up again as Father still watches me from Son's side.

A crowd has gathered to condemn the King. They yell, "Crucify!" "Crucify!" and I am amongst them. Jesus is at the base of a mountain as many are shouting, "Crucify!" I watch in utter disbelief. Is this my mouth that has joined their screaming? Jesus sits at the base of a mountain, teaching, imploring, calling their names, yet, in the truth of what He spoke, they take offense. They so deftly reply, "Guilty!" Guilty sets off an avalanche, the boulders so huge with the rocks of offense. Jesus, guiltless, truth, of pure intent, lifts up His eyes to heaven, "Friends, apostles, disciples, man; surely one must hear My heart. I mean no harm." Yet in Jesus' darkest hours of need, only Fear didst add to offense's weight.

"Crucify, crucify!"
and beneath each rock, each stone, each cry,
Jesus is meant to die.

At first the blows of betrayal's breath did sting.
Jesus, thinking inside,
"Was it not with thee
I didst just sup and dine?"
Another rock, another stone hurled to bury truth with lies.

As the accusations came,
those He knew and loved, and played,
buried love for their greater gain.

He longed to assure them, "It is not I that stand as your accuser. I AM heaven's door.

Come, come up here, to chambers sweet and whispers true."
"Crucify Him! Crucify!"
Their only response, blinded by fear, blinded by lies.
"Oh God, I am guilty!" drowns out my own heart's cry.

"I'm guilty. I'm sorry! Oh Father, What have I done?" For the first time I knew someone hurt more than I, and I was glad. I took the strips of flesh and laid down to rest. "I'm sorry. I'm so grateful for Your pain. I accept Your offering. Is there a bandage for the heart shame?"

"Look deeper," the Father answers me,
and takes my face past muscle and bone.

I thank Him
and He carries on.

Past bone and marrow, into the center of Christ's flow,
I suddenly see a brilliant, snow white living river.

In the middle of the marrow of His deepest price,
somehow I knew this was the final answer to my heart's cry!

The river flowed like diamonds sewn together, infused with every color then set on fire!

"What is this flow?"
"This flow is My Divine nature,
my dear, My DNA, My code."

In Ephesians chapter 2, Father says that even when my nature, my very nature was at enmity with Him, in order to show His great and extravagant love towards me and for me, He resurrected me with His Son and set me in the heavenly realm. In the blood, as the blood of

Love flowed! Love is God, God is Love, and Love is Light. When God chose to place my dark nature in Light, in Jesus, what was stronger? I am, in my carnal nature, unable to love. Yet, He takes me and plunges me into living blood, light, and my darkness is swallowed up in the Light. Darkness never overpowers or puts out the Light! He showed me His Son's flesh, His sinews, His bones, past the marrow of the bone, into a center of living white stream of fire. "Look in the center of the marrow of My Son's Heart." This brilliant flow, so clear, shows forth like lancets of snow in brilliant white, reflecting from the center core a rainbow fire of every color! Like living snow fire, like living opals. Fiery opulence. "What is this flow?" I ask. "My Divine nature," answers Father. "It is where I have placed you, to raise you up with my Son. So, can the lump of coal, what you define as sin in your own life, stand up to the living lava of my Divine nature? No."

> The depth of the gashes of life,
> in Christ, lay bare,
> I am driven to stare.

Not at a mere stripe; but a full-blown bone-exposing, ripped, torn gash in Your body, all the way to the bone. The agony of my desperate cry pales in comparison to the carnage and crimson red guts. Yes guts; spilled out all over. I stare, horrified yet captive. "HERE!" speaks the Father. "What?" I say. "HERE," He replies again. "This is where I put My pain, and here is where I put yours. He lifts up my body and I am placed in the gash of Jesus Christ. I am placed in the question of 'Where did YOU put Your pain?'" He takes my face and places it deep within the wound of Jesus. It's like my face sunk past skin, past muscle and tendons. Past layers of teasing and guilt, past layers of accusations and fear, deeper and deeper I am plunged as the dull reddish tone of flowing blood turns brighter and brighter red. Past beatings and words in body and mind, deep oh so deep as each layer of tendons and torn ligaments cling and fill in the voids of each agony in my body and mind. Blood, living blood cleaning pain's toll, clinging to every vacancy in my being.

"But God – so rich is He in His mercy! Because of and in order to satisfy the great and wonderful and intense love with which He loved us, Even when we were dead (slain) by [our own] shortcomings and trespasses, He made us alive together in fellowship and in union with Christ; [He gave us the very life of Christ Himself, the same new life with which He quickened Him, for] it is by grace (His favor and mercy which you did not deserve) that you are saved [a]delivered from judgment and made partakers of Christ's salvation." (AMP, Ephesians 2:4-5)

A cry so primal now possesses me, a question so real: "I know Your torn and bloodied sacrifice fills in my outside shame; and even to some depth the abuse and cry." "Excuse me if I may ask; WHERE DID YOU PUT THE PAIN SO DEEP, IT SETTLES IN YOUR BONES? Where did You put shame pain? Where did You put rape pain, molestation pain, miscarriage pain; babies who never got a name, and sins-of-the-body-too-bad-to-name pain? Bone pain?" The Lord takes a big breath, then takes me past the bones of His Son that lay so still. Past the marrow that crucified my pain, and in the midst of His marrow I see a pure white flow. I am arrested in the core of my cry, for this stream is pure, white-diamond laced, rainbow and fiery oil-encased stream! A flow like oil and diamonds and fire and life, past the bone; bone oil!

Past bones that hide such shame, now the bones burn with His DNA; Divine Nature Absorbed. The Lord continues to show me more: "And He raised us up together with Him and made us sit down together [giving us b joint seating with Him] in the heavenly sphere [by virtue of our being] in Christ Jesus (the Messiah, the Anointed One). He did this that He might clearly demonstrate through the ages to come the immeasurable (limitless, surpassing) riches of His free grace (his unmerited favor) in [His] kindness and goodness of heart toward us in Christ Jesus." (AMP, Ephesians 2: 6-7) But God who is rich in mercy, for His great love wherewith He loved us, EVEN WHEN WE WERE DEAD IN SINS, hath quickened us together with, (to make one alive together] with Christ, (Strong's #G4862) and has RAISED US UP TOGETHER, AND MADE US TO SIT TOGETHER, IN HEAVENLY PLACES, IN CHRIST JESUS.

So, even when in my nature I was held captive by the dark things done to me, in order for God to show His great and intense love for me, He takes my darkness and places me in His Son. For I cannot be raised together with Him if I am not placed with Him to begin with, and He seats me in the heavenly spheres with Him, His nature, His love.

Now I am at this stream of divine flow past the marrow of His bones. The Father beckons me now to drink. I know not how. So He overshadows me, takes my hands into His, and cups them together to scoop up the precious flow. As the first drops of Divinity's stream enter me, I rest, ceasing from all striving in a peace I have never known. Everything stops except the savor of this sweet liquid in me. Love, Joy, Patience, Goodness, Gentleness, like a fruitful bounty, enter my taste buds exploding and imploding the core of me, in unity, with Jesus Christ. Like liquid clay of His DNA I felt it fill in all voids as scraps of torment are washed through into oblivion, except that which now possesses me; HIM!

He takes some and pours it over me. Like cool, cool clay with Him I lay, cheek-to-cheek in ecstasy. Jesus smiles at me and says, "It's a perfect match." "What" I inquire?" "MY blood stream and your tears, as forms of DNA, join. Now My nature, as the Eternal strand, has absorbed yours."

I ask Him then,
"I have seen my innocence die –
by dark things done to me
and in my sight.
How does this flow of images
stop in YOU, in my mind?"

He brings me to a passage in Ezekiel that states: "And it came to pass, that when he had commanded the man clothed with linen, saying, 'Take fire from between the wheels, from between the cherubim; then he went in, and stood beside the wheels.'" (KJV, Ezekiel 10:6) Jesus said in response to my question, "Take the fire of My purified word in heaven by the angels, and apply it to your eyes. Lift up your eyes." "I will lift up my eyes to the Lord from whence cometh my help." (Psalms 121:1) So I do, I lift my gaze to stare at Jesus. The fire of Him goes into my spiritual eyesight. I can feel it burn my natural eyes, and all images of porn and pain are burnt up in a sweeping blaze. All the images from the time I was molested, till the present are wiped out in a firestorm of epic proportions, and nothing but ashes is left in my mind and heart's eye. Hmmm, "...beauty for ashes..." (KJV, Isaiah 61:3) I see a seed of green rising from the ashes of my being. It grows into a tree. The very tree used for Jesus, yet glory streams through the back of the cross out shining, through my natural eyes, and I can now see all things only through the finished work of the cross. Sight resurrected. This fire forms a firewall around my skull, thus protecting me from all other images.

Oh now I am excited. "My ears, my ears!" I say, "I have heard the most horrible names. My ears, oh Lord...my ears!" The Lords smiles and Jesus takes a cup from His side. "Here, honey, take this and pour it in your ears." I lay my head on Jesus' lap and proceed to do just that. At first I hear like a bird, then humming, and thunder and then a huge trumpet blast. My ears are alive with life and somehow join with the fire sight in my eyes. Living Word. Oh, Lord! He smiles greatly again and said to me, "EYE HAS NOT SEEN, NOR EAR HEARD, NEITHER HAD IT ENTERED INTO THE HEART OF MAN,THE THINGS THAT GOD HAD PREPARED FOR THEM THAT LOVE HIM." (KJV, 1Corinthians 2:9)

"One more thing,
Abuses' mouth has spoken unclean things
that were done to me.

With words I have been slayed
more than physical beatings."

He gently leaned into me and kisses my heart. "O generation of vipers, how can ye, being evil, speak good things? For out of the abundance of the heart the mouth speaketh." (KJV, Matthew 12: 34) So He addresses my heart where the words had landed. "The LORD shall preserve thee from all evil: He shall preserve thy soul." (KJV, Psalms 121:7) The definition of soul found in Strong's H5315 is 'heart'. I now drink deeply again of His flow.

For it is the point of the spear
that opened access here.

So the point of my living stream
is it pierces past all spoken lies,
and lets the river
flow inside.

I drink so deeply and as I imbibe, I sense the cross come and pierce inside my heart. Actually this piercing went through my heart, out the backside, in Christ, yet past His flesh, back to the beginning before the fall of man. I am injected, infused past earthly form, before I was in physical form. In the beginning was the word the word was with God and the Word was God. God made words first. All other abuse or misuse of the words heard must now bow! And I am in the beginning. Born anew!

14

D.N.A.

As soon as I began to grasp this, this fact, this truth, I realize this can consume all my darkness! Light, love, life, His life for mine! And slowly I realize it matters to Him. All along, He knew that I, man, would try to die. He sent His Word before me. "Be still. Be still".

When pain was done
He opened up His Son.

I went into His side,
the open side
of He who had already died.

All my weakness, all my walls of defense of trying so hard not to feel, all is crumbling in amazing surrender. All the separate places, fake faces, and pain; walls of pain. Fortresses of self-preservation, places of refuge inside my being separating mind from thoughts, thoughts from feelings, feeling from body. Just separating so as, so as so, "I don't know" becomes "All knowing, in You". This flows from Your pierced heart, and in so doing, all my fortresses collapse, as I do, into Your immortal stream, Your Divine Nature Absorbed, or better yet, Daddy's Nature Achieved

DNA! Your nature, for mine. Forever complete! Wow!

Where did You put Your Pain? Here, in Your pierced side. Where did You put my pain, my pain of being separate from You, from me, from life, from love? In Christ Jesus. In the Amplified version, Isaiah 53 states, "Surely He has borne our griefs (sicknesses, weaknesses, and distresses) and carried our sorrows and pains [of punishment]..." (AMP, Isaiah 53: 4). Where did You put Your pain? Isaiah continues, "He was wounded for our transgressions, He was bruised for our guilt and iniquities; the chastisement [needful to obtain] peace and well-being for us was upon Him, and with the stripes [that wounded] Him (I am) healed and made whole." (AMP, Isaiah

53: 5). Made whole, made whole. As I pondered my being whole in Him, God continued to show me the depth of His provision through His Son.

He was beaten. He was bruised. He was torn for me. He was made an object of horror as many were astonished at Him. Where did You put Your pain? In the Divine flow of His Son's blood, the stream of love, the river of life carried ALL of heaven's price. How?

"[For many the Servant of God became an object of horror; many were astonished at Him.] His face and His whole appearance were marred more than any man's, and His form beyond that of the sons of men..." (AMP, Isaiah 52:14). His whole appearance was marred, bloodied, beaten, ravaged, shredded, MORE than any man's, and His form, torn beyond that of the sons of men. Beaten beyond me, beyond the sons of men, beyond abuse, rape, agony, myself. Beyond my pain. More than any man, more than any other man... more than more than, more than me... More than ME. More than me. Beyond flesh, pain... beyond doubt. Beyond dark. Beyond. "Let me take you beyond what you are able to think."

"For I am persuaded beyond doubt (am sure) that neither death nor life, nor angels nor principalities, nor things impending and threatening nor things to come, nor powers, nor height nor depth, nor anything else in all creation will be able to separate us from the love of God which is in Christ Jesus our Lord." (AMP, Romans 8: 38)

Nothing can separate us form the Love of God in Christ Jesus. Where did You put Your pain? In love. "For God so greatly loved and dearly prized the world that He [even] gave up His only begotten (unique) Son, so that whoever believes in (trusts in, clings to, relies on) Him shall not perish (come to destruction, be lost) but have eternal (everlasting) life. For God did not send the Son into the world in order to judge (to reject, to condemn, to pass sentence on) the world, but that the world might find salvation and be made safe and sound through Him." (AMP, John 3: 16-17) For God so loved me He gave me... more love. He did not send His Son to judge me, but that I would be saved through Him.

I am persuaded beyond doubt now where He put His pain... in His Son. The question of "Where did You put Your pain?" becomes "In whom did You put 'our' pain?" For me, for you, as this realization took hold of me again and again. Soon I forgot about my question of "Where?" for suddenly I knew there was no shame, no pain, or no game so deep that God's love was not deeper still. Why? Isaiah again answers me in stunned, stark reality. "Yet it was the will of the Lord to bruise Him; He has put Him to grief and made Him sick." (AMP, Isaiah 53: 10). "He shall see the fruit of the travail of His soul (Judas' kiss) and be satisfied; by His knowledge of Himself [which He possesses and imparts to others] shall My [uncompromisingly] righteous One, My Servant, justify many and make many righteous (upright and in right standing with God) with Love." (AMP, Isaiah 53: 11). I can face God and not be apart from Him! For He shall bear my guilt and sin with all my consequences!

Where did He put His pain? In His Son, for me to be able to enjoy, without shame or guilt, the relationship of my heavenly Father again, for me to enjoy love without guilt! I am in such utter shock and gratefulness that I dance with joy! I cry in joy! I sing, "I'm free, I'm free, I'm free to return the love He's given me." I wish to bring Him riches and treasures and grateful praise. Yet, what can I give Him who has everything? I know: I give my heart, unwavering. Like the alabaster box, I offer Him my care, pure in Him. Yet this time I offer it not as a sinner's dark need for light, I offer my heart as an offering of Right; The right to love, the right to be loved, full of Him. In Song of Solomon it says: "Set me like a seal upon your heart, like a seal upon your arm; for love is as strong as death, jealousy is as hard and cruel as Sheol, its flashes are flashes of fire, a most vehement flame, the very flame of the Lord." (Song of Solomon 8: 6).

15

CRUCIBLE OF CHRIST

I touch His face. I know the place. My thumb touches where the thorns did pierce and I cry. Each thorn, each wound upon his head was jammed into place to remove my fear and dread. "Go ahead Cath, take out just one thorn and see." I hold one thorn removed from His brow. As it is removed, resurrection's fire and light come pouring out. He said, "Look at the thorn in your hand." I do. It is cylindrical in shape, a bit hollow, and I question Him with a glance. He smiles and I feel something warm in the thorn in my hand. It is filled with His blood. "This," He says, "is my cup, the Crucible of Christ, for I have taken the cup of suffering from your hands and given it into the hands of your enemies. "Drink deeply of My love, oh precious one, for I know that thou art Mine, irrevocably mine!" (AMP, Song of Solomon 5: 1)

Who could harm Love's price? I am so fully in Him, His love bursting from within. I smile and pat His cheek. My fingers trace where they plucked His beard and the silhouette of time. My heart bursts forth in rapturous adoration. I offer it unto Him as communion from my being. "Take, eat." I say to Him. "Take, eat." And from within my core, I lift my heart, fully white, blazing true, a direct image of the imprint of His glory, pure love. "I offer you, my Jesus, Your love perfected in me, back to Thee. Take, eat, remember me unto Thyself." With tears of joy, Jesus takes my heart, breaks it in half, and has communion with me. Take, eat, do this, offer Me your heart, in remembrance of Me." He takes the one side of my heart; I take the other that He's just offered back to me. Together we stare into each other's core, eat Love's surrendered heart, and as we do, I am possessed by Him and He by me.

There is no distinction for the two halves of my heart, taken together in communion with Him, united within His belly, His chest, His very being, and there is the final union; a heart surrendered, totally in union, undivided.

Inexpressible tears flow freely and as sweet as any costly perfume. His gaze, His face, His love as He now gazes upon me and I on Him. He turns ever so slightly and says, "And now Cathy, you may ask Pain to leave, for you have truly loved me past your own need. You have loved Me for Me. There is no pain, no shame or no game so deep that My love is not deeper still.

Still...Be.

16

LOVE'S SEAL

A miracle?

"Yes," some would say. I just know Christ's love did separate pain

From my body, mind and soul that day!

July 16, 2012, Pain did leave, and Addiction, Withdrawal and Suffering too. Yet, truly it was like an afterthought to me for I only had eyes on the Lord and King. To Him I speak:

Kiss me with Divinity's lips

Linger on, I plead –

Dance upon and draw forth Thy sweet wine –

Lovingly our lips meet: Communion

A thousand times a day –

Divine exchange of His DNA

My thirst and price quenched now –

By Thee and Thine.

Jesus then took a scroll from beneath His feet, handed it to me and gave it to me to read. It said, "You are mine. Complete. Complete. Complete. Done." "Before I formed you in the womb I knew [and] approved of you [as My chosen instrument], and before you were born I separated and set you apart, consecrating you; [and] I appointed you as a prophet to the nations." (AMP, Jeremiah 1: 5).

It is my birthright for accepting God's only Son, for it is how I've overcome.

Come. The next half of the book, "God, where did You put Your reign" is about to begin...

PART TWO

Where Did You Put Your Reign Lord?

DR. CATHLEEN M. SCHMITT

1

COURTS OF GOD'S LAW

Above in love! The Law of the Spirit of life in Christ Jesus has set me free... to be loved, Legally! Wholly!

I am undone and so totally at peace. I sense the need to return this, this right of the light, to be loved. I'm in.

Again, as I offer my heartfelt praise to Him, In worship, in the Spirit, I break my heart as an offering, upon Him, and my tears of joy adorn His feet; Take Jesus, take and eat. Remember yourself in Me – I love you with all of Your heart – Take, eat, remember Me in your love and glory.

We exchange the communion of our love. As I am pouring out of my inner being love to Him in grateful praise, He stops for a moment...

With direct divine intent He returns my stare, my wondrous tears of His love, and says, "And now my love, you may ask pain to leave." For you have loved me beyond your own need." As He speaks I address my body's pain, "You may leave now; job is done". The pain did leave in the authority of the right of me being in the Son, and it does take its leave. Nothing can distract me from Jesus who is before me. Then Jesus reaches for something underneath His feet. It is a rolled up piece of paper, a "policy", a scroll. He hands it to me. The seals upon it have been opened for me. I unfurl its contents. It reads: "You are mine. Complete. Complete. Complete. Done." I stare at Him and He smiles and leaves saying, "Take this, Cathy, to My courts."

I am excited yet stunned. Firstly, I needed to know what this paper was in my hand is. Then, how do I get to heaven's court? I waited in worship before God and asked Holy Spirit, who is Truth and who will bring all things to my remembrance such as I have need, "What is this policy, this testament – that Christ has handed me?" Holy Spirit reminded me and revealed, "Thine eyes did see my unformed substance, and in Your book all the days (of my life) were written before they ever took shape." (KJV, Psalms 139: 16) Okay, a book before I was born... God wrote about me before I was! Then in Jeremiah: "Before I formed thee in your mother's womb, I knew thee, and before you came forth out of the womb I sanctified you, and ordained you a prophet unto the nations..." (KJV, Jeremiah 1: 4)

Ordained: 1. Make a priest or minister; confer holy orders on 2. Order or decree something officially (origin of ordained), to put in order

So, the "policy", or papers Christ handed me, are official papers stating I am His! Before I was born I was His! In fact, to confer means to have discussions, exchange opinions... a title, degree, benefit or RIGHT. In all truth, this "paper" is my birthright as a joint heir in Christ! Before I was born, as I was being formed in my mother's womb, the Lord ordained my life. We had discussions about it and He made it plain for anyone to see in the decree stating, "She ("we") is (was) mine. Again, my RIGHT, which He conferred upon me, as HIS.

2

HIS COURT PROTOCOL

Ah! Now that is an official document worthy of a courtroom appearance! Now I just had to find out how to go to God's court! Again Holy Spirit reminded me of Psalms, "Make a joyful noise unto the LORD, all ye lands. Serve the LORD with gladness: come before His presence with singing. Enter into His gates with thanksgiving, and into His courts with praise: be thankful unto Him, and bless His name." (KJV, Psalms 100:1, 2, 4)

I have papers stating I am His. I have His word that says to come into His presence. How? With singing! (Note: I am not asking God to come down. He says to "Come to me, with singing.") He is LORD. He made me. I am thankful, which gets me "through the security" gate to enter His courts. "What then can we say? If God is for me who can be against me?" (KJV, Romans 8: 31) I now must enter by praise. Praise, in this verse,means 'a loud, sustained, energetic out-burst'.Like the dance of King David!

As I go to enter the courtroom, Holy Spirit whispers to me, "You're not dressed correctly. Lean into Me."

The courtroom bailiff announces, "All rise for His Majesty, the Great I AM. King of kings and Lord of Lords." Enter Abba Father, Lord and King. Enter Absolute Authority. I bow in honor and awe. He is seated. Eternal Judge.

"Prosecution, state your case." From the left side of the courtroom, yet within the seven spirits before the throne, I witness screaming strong! Addiction starts. "She knows my name, and over and over He encountered her, yet morning and evening she'd reach for me." "I know her. I own her. She's already chosen me."

Pain and Suffering chime right in, "She looked to us for sympathy. I gave her the attention she so desperately needs." On and on the accusations flew, and Withdrawal just snickered, "ha, ha, we got you..."

Almighty Judge heard the evidence, and addressing the court asked, "Is there a defense?" The Holy Spirit arises and speaks, He quotes the word in His opening statement: (KJV, Psalms 35: 11, 23, 24) "False witnesses did rise up. They laid to her, (my), charge, things that she, (I), knew not. (23) Stir up Thyself, and awake to her, (my) judgments, even to her (my) cause My God and my Lord. (24) Judge her (me), ACCORDING TO THY RIGHTEOUSNESS and let them not rejoice over her, (me)." His Honor responds, "Call forth your first witness."

From the center of defense, as a great cloud of witnesses arose, father Abraham stood and spoke, "This woman has spoken with me. I have rocked her heart and soul in my bosom, the bosom of Abraham, in order for her to gain an understanding of a father's love. Then she brought nations and sons and kings. If they lacked the love of a father on earth she would carry them in her heart, and bring them here to me."

"Your Majesty, it is as the accuser says. I am guilty. Judge me according to Your mercy.

I'm sorry for my actions."

Moses rose and Abraham sat down. "She used my rod to bring clarity, separating lands of lie from truth." A homeless man, a child, a son, all rose and witnessed of what I had done.

The Judge listened to all the legalities and then He looked and spoke to me. "How then do you plead?"

I leaned into Counsel, Understanding, Wisdom, Knowledge and the Spirit of the Lord. Might upheld me as, with my counsel, I stood to state my plea while the reverential awe (Fear) of God kept me humble. "Your Majesty, it is as the accuser says. I am guilty. Judge me according to Your mercy. I'm sorry for my actions."

Almighty Judge makes a plea, "Is there anyone else who will speak to her defense?" And, from the right, with authority and peace, Jesus responds to the Judge's plea, "I contest on her behalf even her own guilty plea." Jesus steps directly in front of me, blocking the Judge's view, and I am drawn into Him, like a hologram, and as I do a gash of blood, fresh, appears on my heart. The paper testament He gave me from under His feet, that was rolled like a scroll, appears in my heart, comes to my hand which is now one with Jesus' hand, for I am completely hidden and one with Him.

The Judge says, "Present the evidence." Jesus' hand places the paper on the Judge's desk, yet it is my fingers that release its grasp. Jesus' thoughts are now mine and in Him I live and move and have my being.

"Your Majesty," Jesus says, "On the day of the eleventh of February, 1972 she confessed with her mouth and believed in her heart that I am God, and asked me to come into her heart to save her from the guilt of sin. I became her Savior that day. By blood, My body now rules in her as a testimony, for she has been overcome by the blood of the Lamb and the word of her testimony, which I now present to You. Upon her profession of faith in me, by grace she is saved. Yet that is only part. For now I appeal to Your standards of truth which trump the penalty of sin and lies. Your word, Your law, which I came to fulfill, states, 'There is therefore now no condemnation for those who are in Christ Jesus', Me. For the law of the Spirit of Life is in Me and she is Mine, complete, complete, complete and done, has set her free from the law of sin and death. She believed my words over her circumstance, and by this act of faith I present my case."

His Majesty then takes my scroll, the papers, and bends to read. In letters penned by blood it states, "You are mine. Complete. Complete. Complete, Done."

His Majesty the Judge now nods His head, looks to the left and speaks so clearly, addressing the accusers, "Pain, Addiction, Withdrawal and Suffering," He says, "YOUR WORDS HOLD NO WEIGHT IN THIS COURT. For the Law of the Spirit of Life in Christ Jesus has set her free from the law of sin and death."

Then, with massive hands, He grasps the gavel of Righteousness, Justice, and Truth, brings it down on the desk of judgment and "NOT GUILTY" rings out over the courtroom. It is through. NOT GUILTY, NOT GUILTY, NOT GUILTY – the decree, and all of heaven celebrates the victory! (I must mention here that many people stop here, at the 'not guilty decree'. Until a case is closed, however, it leaves one open for other activity. I will explain in detail how this is done in the next segment.)

3

'NOT GUILTY'

In wonder and reverence, I celebrate, too. Then His Majesty, the Judge turns and looks at me. "Approach the bench please." I quickly obey. He reaches out His hand to me, smiling, and says, "Do you want to try on My Judge's robe?" "Father, Father!" I smile so wide, and dropping all pretenses, I rush right up beside Him! "Here. Try it on for size." I did, and the weight was so very, very heavy. I looked in Father's face and the weight lifted just enough to bear the garment. "Now, see here, you must always seek first My kingdom and My righteousness, and all these things shall be added. When your eye is single, your whole body is sound. Sound enough to bear the garment of government." I just stared at His face, absorbed by the weight of His words. I listened intently to Him and soon the garment of government began to get lighter and lighter, almost like my own skin, yet vibrant and heavy in a bearable way. I almost wanted to ask if I was wearing the garment or was this garment wearing me? It seemed like every righteous judge and their decrees were woven into this robe, living testimony, living decrees, in every fiber, filling the all-in-all of me.

I am brought out of this thought by Father's voice. He asks, "Would you like to hold the gavel?" "Oh, the gavel, the gavel," as thoughts race through my mind of "Order in the court! Not guilty!" I fervently answer, "Yes!"

He sits me on His seat of authority so I can see better, hands me the gavel and steps aside. I try to pick it up and am unable to do so. Father smiles. He comes behind me and completely covers me with His body from behind. He reaches His arms around my shoulders, arm to arm. He then grasps my hands in His while I grasp the gavel, and with great ease I lift it high and bring it down again. "Whack! Not Guilty!" It rings with might, "Smack! Not guilty," it rings again. With each loud smack of the gavel's sweet sound, the whack has a power all its own. "Smack" devils cringe. "Smack!" the Father's sound. "Smack, smack, smack, whack" His authority rebounds and rebounds. All authority rings strong and true, absolute power, no war here. Dominion of the Divine! Anything less does bow!

All authority rings strong and true, absolute power, now war here.
Dominion of the Divine! Anything less does bow.

I have leaned back into the chest of Father as the gavel we hold lies still, for the utmost complete stillness in Him is louder than any tone. I rest for a blissful pause, overshadowed in Him. The past is now at rest into absolute peace. There is nothing that gets past my Father's rule, past His great and mighty will for all, for me. Seek ye first the kingdom of God and His righteousness, and all these things shall be added to you.

The right to rule is all-inclusive in Him, through me, for His glory! "Thy kingdom come, Thy will be done on earth as it is in heaven." (AMP, Matthew 6: 9)

Father God is still overshadowing me. Although the gavel is still, I am in perfect peace, just breathing Him. I know He will reveal more to me in the months to come so I do not seek, I rest. All He needs me to understand will come.

You know, there's more! He says to me, "I just trust." He then continues to show me, "The judgment has been rendered 'not guilty' for you, yet your accusers must stand for sentencing. They are judged in their ignorance of My kingdom proceedings, outside of the law of the Spirit of life in Christ Jesus." "How is this judgment carried out, and by whom?" I ask. Father laughs at my quest. "You've seen so much these few days and weeks. Sit with Me for a while and I'll tell you."

I do so and sit and rest in Him without a 'care in the world' (for the Kingdom of God is within).

In the middle of worship Father questions me, "Who carried out my judgments in Sodom and Gomorrah?" "The men in white linen! They did!" I answer. God nods His head with a 'yes.' "All throughout My word My angels have hearkened to the voice of My word." "Bless the Lord ye His angels that excel in strength, that do His commandments, HEARKENING TO THE VOICE OF HIS WORD. Bless ye the Lord all ye hosts, YE MINISTERS OF HIS THAT DO HIS PLEASURE." (KJV, Psalms 103: 20-21) "Yes Lord, Father, yes. Will they serve my accusers the sentence they're due?" I ask Father. "Yes, dearest one. And they will teach you, too."

The men in white linen came along to my left and my right, accompanied with various angels all around and with my birthright in hand we arrive at the sentencing.

Addiction stood like many handcuffs joined together, locked in masse to form a being of sorts. Withdrawal was a smoke-like form. Suffering looked like swollen fruit of some kind, and Pain could have been a human; nothing special to mark its name.

The men in white linen guard me as they approach. I am counseled to just watch this time, and take note. My papers are present in the hands of the men in white linen, and the scroll of heaven is right in mine. Together the men in white linen take God's Word and stick it in the head of each being. Upon impact on Addiction's form, all locks are opened and fall into a heap. The handcuffs interlocked together lie open as God's Word sets me free. Suffering is bloated and explodes like a melon with sticky stuff in bits all around.

Withdrawal, like smoke, withdraws into itself and disappears in a puff of fumes.

Now Pain stands guilty and as the men go to serve it also, I ask to speak. I am granted permission. I let them know Pain was a "friend". Without it, I'd never have known the depths of love and life I now live. The men in white linen just roll their eyes a bit. "My dear, God's love never needs pain. Why, that is the very source of seduction that you've believed all this time! God's love is all in all. You believed you needed pain; it stayed. Deception's game."

In righteous anger I decree, "May I have my papers, please!?" The men nod in agreement and hand me my scroll. I lean into Wisdom and ask, "Where does pain go?" "To the pit of eternal destruction and flames. The truth now binds it with eternity's chains," is their reply. I thrust my scroll so deep into Pain that its countenance goes through an immediate demise. The earth opened

up beneath its feet, into a pit of screaming and flames. Pain was sucked deep inside, screaming and done. The chains of God's Word sealed Pain's fate for good and the earth closed itself back up again.

The men now direct me to collect the evidence of the serving of their sentence. Again I leaned to Knowledge, Wisdom and Understanding and they directed me to take an open handcuff, a piece of Suffering's slime, a puff of smoke and a link of Pain's demise. The first three I did easily. Yet, when it came to pain, I did not want to touch its damned eternal chain. "That's okay," the men said, "We have a spare link". So with evidence in hand we return from heaven's court.

His Majesty, Judge, Father states, "Present the evidence, please." We place the evidence to be examined. Almighty Judge examines the evidence of the sentence served. Smiling, He asks me, "Are there any other petitions concerning this case you would present before this court?" I quickly lean into the seven Spirits before the throne for advice. "Request a divorce, a separation from your accusers," was the unanimous reply. So I do. "Your Honor, I wish to petition the court for a divorce for all agreements and covenants I made with them. I wish to be separated eternally from pain, addiction, withdrawal, and suffering, and the consequences of said agreements. Thereby I request a writ of divorce concerning these accusers, and from any other accusation not founded in Your word.

"And then, according to wise council, I wish to accept the covenant You offer me according to Your word in Ezekiel 16." "First things first," His Honor does reply. He produces the writ of divorce. "Receive this into yourself, that all past treaties and agreements are then null and void. For the law of the Spirit of life in Christ Jesus has set you free from the law of sin and death."

Upon receiving my divorce I ask for a moment of recess. It is granted. I go into my inner chambers and receive the writ of divorce. I take the papers into the chambers of my heart by eating them in the Spirit, in my mouth. As the decree of divorce melted in my mouth, this glorious paper from the Almighty Judge, declaring my emancipation from all my accusers, I wait. As soon as it entered my mouth I could see the words on the paper melting and absorbing all other words. "You will never be well!" – all gone, absorbed into my papers. "You will always have pain, it's just your cross!" – gone. "Come on. Withdrawals will kill ya. Just another one. You can cut down." – gone, gone, gone!

The divorce from God, my Judge, frees me from all the 'I should have, could have, would haves'. All condemnations are absorbed into my paper of divorce. Absorbed: all negative declarations like a huge spongey! My papers settle in my belly. They expand like a huge oasis, with a sweet pool of water. Ahhh, deep, deep waters, streams flow into my veins and arteries and circle around my heart, then shooting up around my head. The block between my heart and mind is now free and great refreshing streams flow freely through me; amazing. "Now when I passed by thee, and looked upon thee, behold, thy time was the time of love; and I spread my skirt over thee, and covered thy nakedness: yea, I swear unto thee, and entered into a covenant with thee, saith the Lord GOD, and thou becamest mine. Then washed I thee with water; yea, I thoroughly washed away thy blood from thee, and I anointed thee with oil." (KJV, Ezekiel 16: 8-9) As His garment,

Himself, covered me, and His covenant consumed me, I am filled up, completely His. His water washes away all clinging mortal blood, all flesh, all shame. I am one in the covenant of His name – now to see the judgment on my accusers!

4

DIVORCE PAPERS

I am caught up in the Spirit to see what happened to my accusers as I received my divorce papers. I see addiction once more, judged. I then see angels that have a key in their hands. The key looks like a nail. A nail, a spike?

The angel approaches addiction, and shows me how it unlocked the arrest addiction had on me. Ahhh! The nails that held Jesus on the cross are the very key that unlocked the handcuffs of addictions form in me!

In fact, the angel smiles and shows me it not only unlocks addiction's chains, the nails that held Christ now unlock any and ALL chains that would keep me bound to earthly law. Then the angel took the point of the nail, impaled addiction's form, and thrust it through the body of Jesus Christ, back to the beginning of time, where there is no addiction or chains, and I am free.

For whom the Son sets free, is free indeed!

Suffering is the next from which I am separated. When suffering exploded like a ripe red melon, I am now shown that the pieces are like chunks of Jesus' body. Parts ripped off as the whips did fly. I pick up pieces of His flesh and apply them to my forehead, and shoulders and body. His body now covers me and "I am crucified with Christ: nevertheless I live; yet not I, but Christ liveth in me: and the life which I now live in the flesh I live by the faith of the Son of God, who loved me, and gave Himself for me." (KJV, Galatians 2: 20) I see all suffering absorbed back to the beginning, through the resurrection, where suffering does not exist. I am seated, and safe, in the heavenly realms.

Now withdrawal, which had withdrawn itself into a puff, it is separated from me by God's original breath. "And the Lord God formed man from the dust of the ground, AND BREATHED INTO HIS NOSTRILS, AND HE BECAME A LIVING BEING." (KJV, Genesis 2: 7) His breath then consumed any vapor that is not sustained by Him, and thus withdrawal is sucked back into the beginning, where it is not sustained. And finally, pain is separated off, divorced, the point of the nails of Christ, to unlock pain's chains, and it was then chained to the pit of eternal damnation.

 I see the Lord, head down the chain, past all fake flames, consuming agonies cry, focused on one intent: to take pain and end its reign; back through dark perception, hell, through the Light of His Word. "In the beginning was the word, and the word was with God, and the Word was God. And the Word is the light that lights the heart of every man." Pain's chains led down to the infernal regions, however, GOD SAID; "and God shall wipe away all tears from their eyes. And there shall be no more death, (the miserable state of the wicked dead in hell) neither shall sorrow nor crying. NEITHER SHALL THERE BE ANY MORE PAIN! For the former things are passed away, BEHOLD, I MAKE ALL THINGS NEW!" (KJV, Revelation 21: 4-5) NO MORE PAIN. NO MORE PAIN. NO, wait, I mean ANYMORE PAIN.

Neither shall there be ANYMORE PAIN. (Anymore means: of a thing which went on formerly, whereas now a different state of thing exists, or has begun to exist.) All things new! All things new!

His Majesty sees it all there, takes the gavel, and once again, "smack!" "It is finished. It is done. CASE CLOSED!"

I am stunned and in awe as I come out of the intense visionary encounter. I take comfort in His Word.

Sometimes I wonder how I can handle the magnitude of such revelation. Paul in Ephesians writes, "For this reason I bow my knees to the Father of our Lord Jesus Christ, from whom the whole family in heaven and earth is named, that He would grant you (us) according to the riches of His glory. To be strengthened with might through His Spirit, in the inner man. That Christ may dwell in our hearts through faith." Why? "That us, being rooted and grounded in love, may be able to grasp, with all the saints, what is the height and depth and length and width the love of Christ, which passes knowledge, that we may be filled with all the fullness of God." (KJV, Ephesians 3: 14)

Yes, this verse helps me to grasp what's just happened; the courts, the love, the Law of the Spirit of Life in Christ Jesus! Your Majesty! And, it also goes on to say that He, God, to Him who is able to do exceedingly abundantly above all that we ask or think, (Amplified Bible: "or even dare to dream!") according to the power that works in us!

To GOD be the glory!

DR. CATHLEEN M. SCHMITT

5

HEAVENLY HOST

Now the magnitude of God's visionary encounters with me were very complex. I was used to His "picture language" yet He knew I needed more help to grasp what I had encountered. As I went up to pray on the mountains across the street from my home, (I called them my "mountain", and still do, when I climb the 800-1000 foot rocks and peaks, when before I could barely walk a straight path, it was and is "my mountain"!!) I would worship and lay... just being with Him, the Lord and remembering His goodness. The heart and court encounters would come back to me and He would clarify details as I revisited them.

I was in such a remembering place in my heart and suddenly an angel appeared. Huge and so lit up with brilliance. The funny thing is he had his hands, each of them, in a defiant stance on his hips. I was so caught unaware and then I smiled within. "Who are you," I asked without speech. "I am Raphael," He answered. A holy hush fell upon me and with His right arm he stepped to the side, made a sweeping invitation and invited me into "somewhere".

As I went at his invitation, I was ushered into the very I AM of my Holy, Mighty Father's soaking presence. Deep, oh so thick and deep, and yet so familiar. Abba Father, Lord King, smiles and says,

"Welcome, to the holy of holies of My heartbeat. You are welcome in Me anytime." Complete rest and absolute awe joined together inside me and I embraced Him yet was embraced in through and unto Him in return. Absorbed, totally absorbed.

Raphael then handed me a cylinder-like container, small, yet full. He said, "Drink this, for this is a cup of vitality. You will drink it as your vital need. This will always cause you to return here, and glancing at Father; in the depths of intimacy." I went to drink, yet having one more question I asked; "Yet, what is it?" Father is pleased, so pleased I ask this of His messenger, "What, I ask is this vitality?" Raphael then answers by showing me what looks like a many-sided, multiple triangle strand coming out of Father's hand. "This vitality is a strand of the divine nature, DNA of your Abba Father, Lord and King."

Truly then, I chose to drink. And all the strength and power of love and peace inside the heartbeat of Father's chest flooded again my entire being. Many times I have imbibed of this immortal flow!

This encounter was followed by many more. Each angel has appeared representing a facet of Almighty God that amplifies itself in my time of desire or need.

A strong angel appeared as I was climbing the boulders on my mountain. I would sometimes look for stronger footholds as I ascended. As usual, I asked him his name. "I am Rocky, for I will set your feet upon the rock of His word as stated in Psalms." "He will give his angels charge over you lest you dash your foot against a rock." (KJV, Psalms 91: 11) He touched my feet and strengthened my ankles, in the physical and in the spirit. I never have fallen in my mountain excursions.

Another angel appeared as a soft yet brilliant glow; warm yet soothing and of course by now my question of 'Who are you?' was usually answered as I enjoyed the encounter. This angel's name is Harmony. With a deep hum that starts at one level tone, and always ends a bit higher on the sound scale, Harmony brings my spirit soul and body into complete harmony with the will of God.

Also, when my body as stiff or aching, I hum in tune with Harmony to the Lord's frequency and immediately my body is in harmony with Him again.

There is Magnify who enlarges God's decrees and Pyro, who is one of my favorites. A messenger of fire who, along with Blaze and Ember, ignites, unites, and relights the ever-living burning desire of Father's love to me. Pyro loves to blow up mindsets that are strongholds against God. Blaze purifies the atmosphere inside my head and melts worry and stress. Ember is a torch in my eye that causes me to burn and blaze for

Almighty Father Lord and King's gaze first and foremost. Fortify is a fort building fortress within my core that establishes boundaries against intruding forces. Along with Militia and Archers, they are line-of-defense angels given to me in times of great persecution.

The archer angels have bows and arrows pointing out and they encircle my heart and shoot for the will of God as they hit targets aimed at my

heart's focus. Militia establishes governmental standards as Sabre, one of my favorites, uses the front incisors from the Lion of Judah and with the dripping spit of the DNA still on the sword's tooth, he waylays any identity issues – for I am the Lord's and His alone!

Oracle, angel of divine utterance, causes one to speak God's word in authority. Revel has a honey wax. When applied to the legs, it caused me to stand under what God reveals. Marvel arrived to handle the marvelous wonders and the emotions that would usually block His encounters.

Fury or Furious is absolute fuel to scream the depth of my love toward Almighty God in absolute passion as Stir continues to stir up, stir up, and stir up such passion!

Medic and Nurse tend to the inside and outside need of spiritual and physical misalignments, as Dignity causes me to arise, sit upright in a dignified position, accepting the magnitude of who I am in God. Allegiance keeps the pledge of my core in strict response to Him and Him alone. All these angels are on call to allow my journey to be one of purpose and to the glory of God!

In March, I was introduced to a Special Forces angel. My mother, whom I loved so, so dearly, had suddenly passed away. The words 'grief and sorrow' don't even touch such a loss. I ached just to call her one more time.

In the first week of my loss, I went to pray in a bit of forest near my home. I sat in the leaves and wept deeply, oh so deep, allowing the groan that even Jesus felt deep within Him before He raised Lazarus, to have its time. Tears pouring from my face, I am all of a sudden visited by one of the most beautiful, huge, iridescent, gigantic angels ever!

His wings are like mother of pearl, windows of liquid-paned glass, living pearl, fire glowing, in absolute stunning bliss. Yet even in this display, his eyes were even more captivating. It is like every moment of every dream, every butterfly or hummingbird wings. Every smile of every being was in these eyes. Stunned, of course, I asked, "Who are you?" "I am Demise," he responds so deep and strong. "Would you like to see how your mother died?" "Demise, Demise; why that means death? You're not, you're not, you CAN'T BE, why?" "Yes," he answers. "I can be and I am." Demise means death, yes, but it also means to transfer from one state to another. "For those who love God I appear as you see me now, ranging from a soft breeze, to colors, or knowing peace; to full blown trances and rapturous glory. However, trust me, I am as dreadful and ominous to those who have not the love of God in their hearts as I am stunning here. Now, I ask again, would you like to see how your mother died?" "Of course I say, "Thank you, carry on."

He then asked me to look momentarily into his eyes. I did. Suddenly the memory of my first child flooded my entire being. Joy and focus as nothing else existed around me, for I was in that moment, captured, captivated by a moment I thought I'd never have. The forest, leaves nor even I existed in that moment. Only the memory that I was now a mother, and here was my first born son. Demise spoke, "Enough, now. Look away." As hard as it was, I quickly and immediately obeyed. He then spoke, "Just as you were caught up in love, in an absolute memory of pure innocence, momentarily, so your mother gazed into my eyes also. As she stared, all of a sudden her children's voices, 'Mom, Mommy, Mother', who she had lost as babies, called her name. Oh, the joy of her heart did soar as their voices beckoned her deep beyond the point of no return in my stare. Do you think she ever felt the disconnect as I cut the cord of mortal life when she answered them there?" "No," I somehow mumbled within my being.

Demise continues, "She never felt her body's loss; never knew, but love had called. She answered with her mother's heart and never looked back again."

I am stunned (weeping and shaking as I write) and He smiles and fades from view. I am so shocked yet notice there are two ants walking on my left hand. I lift up my hand and speak to the ants, "My mother is in heaven. My mother is in love. Oh my Heavenly God, I am talking to ants!!" It doesn't matter. I'm gone. I gently shake them off and stumble home. My mom! My Mom didn't die, she just become one with her Maker's cry. "I love you Ruth, come home." And she did.

In Hebrews the word states: "Are not all angels ministering servants sent to those who will inherit salvation?" (KJV, Hebrews 1: 14) In fact it says, "Are they not all ministering spirits..." which is a reference to His angels. In the Strong's concordance of the Bible, under G3011, 'ministering' means: To be a public servant, obey, relieve, to do a service; perform a work. An angel: A messenger, envoy, one who is sent; a messenger from God.

These messengers from God relieved many areas of my personal life. I had been on drugs and in pain for so long, even dealing with normal emotional occurrences didn't happen. Say the dog got sick. It would need medicine, vet, whatever... I would just be so high, or numb, I would function at the basic level, but not engage the emotions attached with it. Numb, anesthetized, no base for any coping skills – just pills or praise. Right. So as I came home from three weeks of sobriety, yet sober in the body and emotions, too, I only knew God. I didn't know how to cope with feelings that were now 'unleashed'. I prayed for 5-6 hours a day and had peace, great peace.

So, as God started having angels show up, I was able to delegate functions to them that most people take for granted. My angel Focus would cause me to focus on the tasks at hand. Fortify, Militia and Magnify would group my tasks for the day and I could categorize their assignments as needed. Did I start out doing this intentionally? Absolutely not. Remember—my mind had been used to functioning at many different levels at one time before the fullness of unity in God. So as the angels started to appear it was just as natural to use them as they appeared. I'd used God as an escape; now I could employ His messengers sent to 'me' to cope, enjoy and engage the reality of life not numbed with drugs. I have now a beginning grasp of how the government of peace must operate in heaven. I know it has operated great peace in my life and circumstances.

6

ANGELS COMMISSIONED

For the past two years and counting now, I had enjoyed and been awed with the angelic revelation of God's divine nature. Remember, as I had stated before, I did not get captivated by the angel itself or what it brought me: Ointments, scrolls, cups. The point of the ointment for my legs was to stand up under the revelation of God's majesty, to drink for strength to bear and convey the depths of His love and law; the law of the Spirit of Life in Christ Jesus.

The point of God's angels appearing is to always reveal more of Him to us, and reveal more of us to Him.

Now, I was content to just keep meeting the angels and going about God's business till a certain day in June, before my mother died, she started to tell me and my brothers and sisters that she had to have surgery. As it turned out it was a complete procedure called a whipple procedure

– to save a person's insides from cancer; pancreatic cancer. I was, of course, immediately alert and sought God's will on the matter. I asked, "Do you want her now? What is your will?" God answered and said, "Not right now. I need you to send the angels." I said, "What?" He answered and said, "They have oils and swords and drinks of vitality that have helped you, yes?" "Why yes Almighty God, yes." He said, "Well, send the prayer to do the same thing over your mother." In the Basic English Version of the Bible it states: "Give praise to the Lord, you His angels, who are in great strength, doing His orders and waiting for His voice." (BBE Psalms 103: 20) In the KJV, it says: "That do His commandments; harkening to the voice of His word." (KJV, Psalms 103: 20) Harkening: Hear; listen, obey, to hear intelligently, often with implication of attention, obedience, etc. (Strong's H8085)

So as God asked me to send the angels over my mother, I did. They, the angels, are waiting the commands of God; God gave the angels to us. Aren't ALL angels ministering servants, sent to those, us, who will inherit salvation? The angels hearken to God's word. My mouth speaks God's commands. God is not commanding them. I am. He gave them to me! I speak God's word and they obey, to do HIS will on my behalf. Oh, wow!

As I then went into prayer for my mother, I was able to manage the angels in administering the limited understanding I had of them for mom. Yet, oh, how it worked! Revel, who had the honey wax like ointment for strength in my legs, applied the ointment all over Mom so her body would hold up under the surgery. The angels who had cups of light, swords to separate dark from light, oils and ointments galore made it all available to me. Angels Medic and Nurse carried out an operation like never before! I was caught up for hours leading and being led in what to do. How amazing it is to not just 'have random requests to heavenly faith'. Yet to employ and enjoy the government of what He had already allowed and for which he had given me dominion!

"But your Mom died," one could say. Yes that is true, yet allow me to share with you the 3-4 months of health she enjoyed before she died! It, now knowing what we know of her surgery and death, was impossible and miraculous! These details are also from my sister Chris, who being a professor of nursing, unfortunately, knew the medical facts that should have happened immediately afterward. This, however, is how it happened for my mom.

A whipple procedure is a delicate and involved surgery to treat pancreatic cancer. During the operation, the head of the pancreas, bile duct, gall bladder, stomach and bowel, are removed, redirected and then reattached. The after effects of a successful surgery are: weight loss, diarrhea for up to three months, not being able to eat except for small amounts, weakness fatigue and stomach problems. It does, however, supposedly extend one's life.

The surgery at the bare minimum is 4-5 hours. Now, my Mom was 81 at the time, with a pace maker. For her to even be eligible for this surgery was a miracle.

On the day of surgery, my youngest sister Cecilia, and Chris went to wait as Mom went in. Three hours later, the doctor came to speak with them. Chris assumed Mom had possibly passed away, yet the doctor said, "We're done." What? Already miraculous! He continued to say they only had to take 5% of certain organs, like her stomach, and she did amazing! And for the next few months, that was the story. Mom healed then drove, got together with most of my brothers and sisters and their children and grandchildren at my brother Ben and his wife Sylvia's house. There, my mother ate, played, spoke, laughed and enjoyed herself. Complications, yes – some, but to have the ability to do, walk, eat and enjoy a BBQ was a miracle! In fact my sister, Chris who had prepared everyone for the real facts of what Mom would be like after, was as shocked as anyone, as were mom's doctors. She drove, played, laughed and ate. The last pictures her were of fun at a BBQ picnic. Astounding. Ohhh, yes, God's angels, God did miracles. For Mom truly lived in the months before her dying. When she was suddenly gone, 'suddenly' was soon turned to wonder as to how she even made it as long as she did. We knew all of our prayers were heard – from my oldest sister Cyndi to Chris, Brian, Barry, Ben and Cecilia. The angels had lots to do, and I learned to assign them as God would say.

DR. CATHLEEN M. SCHMITT

7

I AM HIS VOICE

As my pastor would go on mission trips, I was awakened in the night to send forth the angels to establish perimeters. Again, I had no idea how, God just asked me, "If you were on an army base camp, how is the base camp set up?" "Then assign angels as the soldiers. They are for me, on his behalf. Guards at the gate, special forces on the outside protecting the walls, lookouts, snipers, sure shots, guards and officers of various ranks and status. The Lord said, "Cath, you don't even have to know their names, just address them in My authority and they will hearken." So I did.

Atmosphere angels clear the atmosphere of any interference when His words go forth. Ministering angels convey His message deep within each hearer of the word. Then there are Defender and Militia angels surrounding the base of where he is traveling – keeping all intruders out. Angels... guide, guard, uphold and keep the glory of God clearly as his rear guard.

There is much more yet this is enough. The personal ways one can thank God for all the angel's work is astounding.

I would like to mention here that all of the angels mentioned in these pages are actually not "mine". I have just been allowed to become so dependent on God, He knew I needed them. Can you, the reader, use these angels? Yes, allow me to unfold His word.

"Bless the Lord ye His angels that excel in strength, that do His commandments; Hearkening to the voice of His word." 'The voice of His word' from Strong's H6963, means the sound, cry, noise, proclamation, sing, song, spark, thunder, yell. Verse 22 continues "Bless the Lord all His works in all places of His dominion. Bless the Lord oh my soul." (KJV, Psalms 103: 20) When He speaks through my mouth, I am His voice!

His works? His dominion? His voice? How? Allow the Holy Spirit to reveal the pure foundation that God has already laid. He will assure you that you, yes you, can and have the right to use His angels. For God uses our mouth to command.

"God said, 'Let us make man in our image, our likeness and let them have dominion over the fish of the sea, and over the foul of the air, over the cattle and over ALL the earth, and over EVERY creeping thing that creepeth upon the earth.'" He made us in His image and likeness and HE let us have dominion! (KJV, Genesis 1: 26) The angels hearken to His word in all places of His dominion! Yes! We are in the earth, in His likeness with all dominion! His likeness, His image? Did He use angels? Hmmm let's see; and what image do I have of Him? Do I think of Him as a child in a manger? Or do I think of Him only on the cross, broken and crucified? "And from Jesus Christ, the true witness, the first to come back from the dead, and the ruler of the kings of the earth..." (BBE, Revelation 1: 5)

Now this was the Jesus fully resurrected. He's Lord over all the kings of the earth? Lord means owner! So as Lord, there must be laws. Laws that lord and govern. What laws? You cannot be a "landlord" without rules and rental agreements, contracts between the two parties. Jesus is "land" Lord over all the earth, all the kings. What are His agreements?

In Joshua it states; "This book of the law shall not depart out of thy mouth; but thou shalt meditate therein day and night, that thou mayest observe to do according to all that is written therein: for then thou shalt make thy way prosperous, and then thou shalt have good success." (KJV, Joshua 1: 8) The law is His word, yet many say, "That was in the Old Testament and only for them." However, in Matthew it states, "Think not that I have come to destroy the law, or the prophets! I am not come to destroy, but to fulfill." (KJV, Matthew 5: 17)

Now, we have been made in His image, the image of Lord over all the kings. Given dominion, God's original design, we can therefore release His angels who wait to hear His voice. This is done because we were made in Jesus' image, by believing in Him. "For God so loved the world that He gave his only begotten Son, that whosoever believeth in Him should not perish, but have everlasting life." (KJV, John 3: 16) We can enjoy the angels as He did!

John states, "And He saith, 'Verily, verily, I say unto you hereafter ye shall see heaven opened and the angels of God ascending and descending upon the Son of Man!'" (KJV, John 1: 51) "And it was there in the wilderness, forty days, tempted of Satan, and was with the wild beasts, AND THE ANGELS ministered unto Him." (KJV, Mark 1: 13) "The son of Man shall send forth His angels." (KJV, Matthew 13: 41) Amazing. Heaven opened for the angels to come up and down after great temptation and in the wilderness they ministered to Him. Then He sends them forth! We have the authority in His image to do the same! So now let us use what God has so readily provided. Are not all angels ministering servants sent to those who will inherit salvation!

I would like to mention another fact here. I happen to love names and God has given me the name of a few of His angels. However it is more important to use them than to know their names. Let me explain…

It is sad that one of my friends has a son who ran away from home, got into trouble and landed in jail. She bailed him out of trouble many times, prayed, talked and counseled him, but he then did it again and now he's in prison. She is tired, has a life of her own, is exhausted because court, tears and dreams of how it was supposed to be. She is so tired she has no time for "names" of angels. So the Lord let her know to categorize the angels for her son. Company of Angels I, please tend to my son's heart. Company II, go to usher in the perfect will of God in the courts. Company of Angels III, tend to his physical protection while in jail. The angels hearken to the voice of His word, not only their names! God said, "Call them angel 1, 2, 3, or a, b, c... whatever works... just send them, use them, release them according to My word. My word from YOUR mouth! It's not hard!"

8

WITHDRAWALS

To grasp the all-in-all of His love, above all I can think, Wow! Above! I am so overcome in the natural that the sound of praise flows from my belly as an outlet and testimony unto God. Like the sound of His gavel, inside me I bend in utterances of "Roooahhh, Roooahhh, Roooahhh!" contracting in my belly and tongue. Like a roar deep within me, this sound continues for over an hour. Even then, after a small break, I am overcome again and again by this wonderful sound.

In Romans it says, "And in the same way the Spirit is a help to our feeble hearts: for we are not able to make prayer to God in the right way; but the Spirit puts our desires into words which are not in our power to say..." (BBE Romans 8: 26) He helps us in our weakness for we do not know how to communicate (pray) to God. The Holy Spirit does this. He bears, helps, comforts me in my weakness, with GROANINGS THAT CANNOT BE UTTERED, and pleads on my behalf with unspeakable yearnings and groanings that are too deep for words!

I groan, I groan, I groan, "Roooahhh, Roooahhh, Roooahhh!" with the Spirit of God helping me in my weakness to hold such revelation of His love, His rule. Now this must be manifest in my body, physically, on earth as it is in heaven. Thy Kingdom come and will be done in me as it is, as I am, in heaven.

Even as this was happening, the pills are still in my body. I am so grateful for the groaning, for now what was revealed in the Kingdom of heaven 'which is at hand' (Mark 1: 15), must now be manifest within me in the Kingdom of God within. Luke 17: 21 reads, "Faith without works is dead." And, God, in His infinite wisdom, opened up my understanding of His love.

Now the time to physically walk out what He showed me all these days is upon me.

Whose report will I believe?

Reference for Oxycodone Withdrawal

Every human being possesses unique DNA, which means, among other things, that they metabolize (organically process and get rid of) every substance that enters their bodies differently. Two people taking the same dose of the same narcotic might experience withdrawal completely differently. In the case of oxycodone withdrawal, for example, one might feel uncomfortable, while the other goes through hell.

For what it's worth, here are some common oxycodone withdrawal symptoms:

Early Signs and Symptoms:

Anxiety
Increased respiratory rate
Sweating
Lacrimation (tearing or crying)
Yawning
Rhinorrhea (runny nose)

Piloerection (goosebumps)
Restlessness
Anorexia
Irritability
Dilated pupils (larger than normal pupils)

Advanced Signs and Symptoms:
Insomnia
Nausea and vomiting
Diarrhea
Weakness
Abdominal cramps
Tachycardia (rapid heartbeat)
Hypertension (abnormally high blood pressure)
Muscle spas
Muscle and bone pain[3]

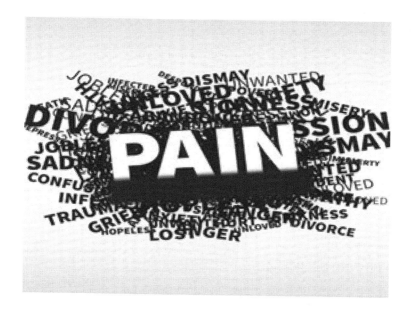

DR. CATHLEEN M. SCHMITT

9

DIVINITY ABSORBING CARNALITY

I am taking eight Percocet, plus six Morphine a day, just to be able to walk. Now I must deny my flesh and walk by FAITH, not by sight. He now will finish what He began. My scroll does not say "Addict". It is storming outside and I have a pill stash in my pockets. I draw from within and remember His face. I take the pills and throw them in a huge water puddle. They disappear. It has begun...

About 24 hours later I ask my most precious friend (in whose house I was staying) to sit with me. This was it, and through 12 straight hours of withdrawal pangs, she wiped my head and hummed His name. Each wave of drugs coming out of me was met with the sound He gave to me, "Roooahhh, Roooahhh, Roooahhh" until in minutes it would pass. His roar of the Spirit of Life in Christ Jesus was stronger than my body's past! Through sweat and gripping, roar and tears, Jayme stayed by my side, cool washcloths on my brow, and the strongest quiet I'd ever known. She just hummed and the wave would pass.

Around the eleventh hour, I felt I couldn't go on. But Jayme would remind me that I couldn't but He can. From 7 p.m. until 7 a.m. the pang and roar did wreak. Then, at hour 12, I felt something leave and only sound remained. There was no pain. Now I fitfully rested for

God spared me great pain. It was not painful in the sense of bone pain. I was in a car accident and was scheduled on August 15 for a complete knee replacement. My knee did not hurt. My bones did not ache. These withdrawals were from my muscles, yet the very bones which were to be replaced did not ache. It is why I choose the word "pang", horrible pangs, gripping contractions. Yet I knew Christ was in my being. I knew He was deeper in me than my bones. Yes, past my bones. He was truly in the middle of my marrow. His DNA (Divine Nature Absorbed) ruled even this withdrawal process. It hurt, yet I was not in pain, I was in Him. It's hard to explain.

Then, withdrawal pangs would come in waves, like inside-out bugs in my muscles trying to get out all at once. Inside-out "itches". To a lesser degree than the first twelve hours? Yes, yet still, for three days this went on. Only the truth of Holy Spirit and His might in my weakness caused me to overcome. Hot baths would help, yet the Lord would remind me of Him, and I would remember the courts, accusers, and especially His loving face. For fourteen days, the flesh did cry with stomach-aches and puking. I was drained. Yet, the sound of "Roooahhh" inside overrode as I remembered Him, as He remembered me.

I couldn't eat anything for days and I asked Him what I should do. God answered and said, "If I send you to the starving you'll have the answer for them, too. I am El Shaddai, the many breasted one. Drink the milk of my word inside." So weak in the flesh yet roaring in the Spirit, my appetite through Him was satisfied. As I drank the literal milk of the Word I could see it restoring my cells. Soon after this I could finally hold down broth. My stomach had stopped cramping! I was sustained! Three days later the Lord said, "Now, draw honey from the Rock." (A metaphor of drawing from Jesus, the Rock of my salvation). After eight or so days I could have some real honey. All the while His 'milk and honey' kept me going.

Each day was like three for I rarely could sleep. This was when the Lord would say, "Remember me." So I would turn my thoughts to Him and He would be my rest, coming to me in pictures and sounds. After two solid weeks I was becoming strong, but, "Not by might, nor by power but by My Spirit saith the Lord." (KJV, Zechariah 4: 6)

"Remember Me," He would continue to say and I would take communion many times a day using water as wine and a bit of cracker.

In John, Jesus said, (reminded me), "I am the Bread of Life. He who comes to Me shall never hunger, and he believes in Me shall never thirst." (KJV, John 6: 20) This truly became real for me. As the strength of my flesh took time to heal, the might of Holy Spirit, Jesus, the Bread of Life was more than my body's need for 'toast'. I became stronger and stronger as each day passed by. My heart would race dramatically when I realized that it was clean, free from pills. God had already showed me how to rest on His chest and match the rhythm of my heart to the rise and fall of His breath. Instantly my heart would be still.

DR. CATHLEEN M. SCHMITT

10

LET THERE BE…

Day by day I was exchanging God's thoughts for mine, remembering His name, and, truly, my body was separated out unto Him, in the sound, the "Roooahhh", always deep inside. He shared with me why this sound overcame my flesh's weakness. God said, "This sound in you is not travail. It is not so much a groan. This sound is a tone of the frequency I used when in Genesis, I formed everything. In Genesis it states, 'In the beginning God created the heavens and the earth. The earth was without form, and void; and darkness was on the face of the deep. And the Spirit of God was hovering, brooding, over the face of the waters.' Then God said, 'Let there be light; and there was light.' (KJV, Genesis 1:1-2) This sound, Cathy, separates the darkness from the light within you. Just like the face of the deep, and void, My Spirit dwells within you, to brood and form from the void of your flesh, light."

"Let there be light," I said. I said. When I spoke I did not use a language of, let's say, English. No, this word 'said' means an ever-increasing crescendo of sound. It means sound. When I speak it is a sound. "When I gave you the 'roar' inside, this sound separates light from the dark within you. It is a sound of creation. It will be with you forever, and I shall use it for others soon. For now, know it forms my light. Let there be light, even in darkness and void! And God said!" And God said it was done. Yet really, it had just begun. My body adjusted more to His sound as I spent hours just praising and singing. There was always a choice that could be made in the followings from the drugs leaving my body. If my muscles would cry out with cramps I would sound forth His 'Word'. It is a choice, a real choice, whether to listen to the cry of my flesh or turn towards His truth.

"Roooahhh, Roooahhh", again, and again. Hot baths, songs of deep worship, and time, much time, spent with Him. He was forming light from the void of Pain's toll, light from the face of the deep called Addiction. Light came from nothing, to form Himself in me. John 1: 1 states, "In the beginning was the Word (Sound), and the Word was with God, and the Word was God. He was in the beginning with God. All things were made through Him, and without Him nothing was made that was made. In Him was life, and the life was the light of men. And the light shines on in darkness, and the darkness did not overcome it. He (Jesus) was in the world, and the world was made through Him, and the world did not know Him. He came to His own, and His own did not receive Him. But as many as received Him, to them He gave the right to become the children of God. To those who believe in His name; who were born, not of blood, nor of the will of the flesh nor of the will of man, but of God."

Our rights as children of God, the right of the Light is mine! Jesus is the Light. Jesus is Love. The right to rule over darkness, the right of light, and the rights of the Law of Life are mine! "For there is therefore now no condemnation for those who are in Christ Jesus."

(KJV, John 1: 1, 4-5, 12-13) "For the law of the Spirit of life in Christ Jesus has set us free from
the law of sin and death." (KJV, Romans 8: 1-3)

"For God did not send His Son into the world to judge the world, but that the world, through Him, might be saved." (KJV, John 3: 17) This right is to as many as receive Him and believe in His name (His Nature)!

11

BEFORE THE REIGN

What drove me to be in Colorado, at Jayme's house? God had told her to fly me over for a few (5 1/2) weeks. Yet, I have responsibilities. I have three grandchildren, a husband and three sons. Two of my sons live with me, the father of my three grandchildren and my oldest son. My youngest son had moved out a couple months prior to my departure.

At the time of my friend asking me to come away, it seemed impossible that I could go. Not known to me, she asked my oldest son, Lawrence, "If I take your Mom for a few weeks, can you hold down everything here?" He said, "Yes. At all costs take my mom, please. If you don't, it will be too late." This may seem like a natural, easy answer, yet my oldest son is from a previous relationship. My firstborn and my husband rarely get along. Besides this, my second oldest son, Stephen, was in the cycle of addiction to alcohol, and, having the grandchildren with me, I assumed they were totally safe. How could I throw him out for drinking when I myself did pain killers? And, if I were to throw him out where would the grandbabies live for his half of the divorce custody arrangements? The anger and frustration of my husband towards Stephen was misplaced in fits of rage, directed mostly at me. When I wasn't there, Lawrence would catch the full brunt.

At this same time, Lawrence had been reunited with his (and her) first love, Sarah. Yet, Lawrence says to my friend, "Yes Jayme, take my mom." This was like saying, literally, "Yes Jayme, I'll take on all this, which I didn't create. My mother's tolerance and denial did. But, yes, take her." It is to this day the most selfless act I've witnessed. My son was laying down everything; safety, go-between, all. And Sarah! She didn't sign up to baby sit, with the ups and downs of three children, (grandbabies 3, 4 and 6 years old) let alone their father Stephen, with his emotional toll of various influences which made him tired, happy, angry, or just wasted at any given moment.

If it were not for Lawrence, I could never have gone to Colorado. He took all my messed up responsibilities as his own. "Just go Mom. Just go." He gave everything humanly possible, even explaining to Sarah what he had to do. Lawrence had come to live with us six months prior, he had been let go from his job because of the economy. He supported my youngest son while he healed from the emotional journeys brought on by a mother who preached Christ and love, yet sold, stole and lived to stay out of pain through drugs. Mixed with severe discord, unworthiness and control, one can only imagine the toll it took on him.

In the six or seven months Lawrence lived with us, he looked every day for a job. When he arrived, he had paid everything up-front for 2 1/2 months, for part of the rent, electric and cable. Yet the money soon ran out. Now he had no job whereas he had worked and been independent for years, and now had to depend on "dad" who was on a limited income. He had to listen to emotional snide remarks that were given whenever possible. I am not oblivious to these things. I usually caught the brunt of it for I would always defend, protect and try to keep my sons from punching my husband for his remarks. (I'm not judging here. I'm just giving some background because of the amazing way God has answered and miraculously blessed our family is worth the foundation of ugly facts.) Lawrence and Sarah gave so much! (At the time of the writing of this book they have just married!) Last Mother's Day, I asked Lawrence about some things. He had found a job. It was a great, high paying, impossible-to-get-hired job without knowing someone on the inside (he knew Jesus), which had a starting pay at twice the minimum wage requirement at the time. I asked him why – when he finally could have moved out of the chaos and hell of abuse from dad, and the emotional tirades from me – why he didn't just take the first chance and run? He stated, "I asked God if there was more that He wanted me to do here. God said, 'You have a choice, Lawrence. You have done everything I've asked of you and you can leave with no condemnation, no looking back, and full of blessing.'"

Lawrence pressed into the Lord further asking, "Is there more Lord?" God then showed him two choices. If he left right then he would be blessed. Truly so, but his family's trials would last longer. Yet, if he chose to stand and sacrifice the very peace and safety of life away from home that the Lord had just monetarily given to him through his job, his family's trials would be shortened as he 'stood in the gap'. Two roads. Two choices. For Lawrence, there were no consequences to be had either way. He had already been the sacrifice of my husband's abuse for thirty years. He was not my husband's blood, and our unspoken connection, Lawrence's and mine,

---

"Save yourself. The others will survive. Come on, you've done your part; way more than anyone else could. Get out. It's over."

---

was blood deep, and it threatened my husband just by its existence. Lawrence had been sacrificed. He was done – and God would bless him. Yet he told me that the true, deep glory of God, to see it, and have it manifest in miracles, signs and wonders always requires a sacrifice, just like his Son Jesus. And the only sacrifice pleasing to God is 'self will'. Self Will.

"Save yourself. The others will survive. Come on, you've done your part; way more than anyone else could. Get out. It's over." Yet for everything that screamed inside to 'go', the extra something that wanted the 'All of God' stayed. Stayed home, stayed in violent faith, stayed for us, his family. He then had to tell Sarah, "Honey, I've got to do this." It's one thing for a son to stay. It's another thing for a fiancé to watch him give himself time and time again for something God told him that, on the outside, looked like suicide. As he told me this just recently, I had more respect and awesome love for my now daughter-in-law, for her faith in God. She stood with her promised husband-to-be, gave up more of her time with him and their loving moments, to see this family's trials shortened. "Who cares Lawrence!" you would have thought she'd scream. I'm sure it crossed her heart in her love for him. Yet she believed God spoke and she, too, stood firmly on God's plan.

Yes, Lawrence and Sarah laid their hope in Christ's pattern of sacrifice. In Romans 8 it states, "For all creation was subject to futility and frustration. Not by any fault of its own, but for a greater hope by the will of He who subjected it: That creation itself will be set free from its bondage to decay and corruption, into the glorious freedom of God's children." Wow! Now, does this mean Lawrence was perfect? "Oh, now I'm going to be the sacrifice" with a "holier than thou" attitude? Give me a break! There was so much anger and frustration in the out-working of God's promise to him. Romans 8, the scripture I just quoted, spoke of futility and frustration, yet for the greater hope.

God had spoken. The rest was up to Him, to God, the greater hope in spite of what is seen? Have faith: the substance of things hoped for, the evidence of things not seen. Yet the frustration and futility through the journey, with the hope as an anchor, caused outbursts of rage. Does a lamb or an ox that is to be sacrificed just lay there as its throat is cut? No! It moves violently until it dies, subject to futility and frustration.

Futility means: The quality of producing no valuable effect, or of coming to nothing; as the futility of measures or schemes. (Webster's Dictionary) Frustration means: Literally, to break or interrupt; hence, to defeat; to disappoint; to balk; to bring to nothing; as, to frustrate a plan, design or attempt; to frustrate the will or purpose. (Webster's Dictionary)

Lawrence was subject to arguments, reactions to circumstances, out-workings of the inner rule that came as he said to the Lord; "I choose to sacrifice my comfort at this moment for Your greater will for all, not just me." The priest in the Old Testament would take the sacrificial sheep, cut its throat, hang it upside down and remove its guts. He would then skin it, remove its head, legs and all of the muscle to access the ribs.

It is surrender to Christ from Lawrence (or us) to exchange Jesus' life for his own. Once the choice was made by Lawrence, it was then the High Priest (Jesus') job to make sure that Lawrence was stripped enough of his own self-will to be exchanged for the will of the Lord. The heart, the kidneys, all was exposed to God, exposed to the glory of the kingdom so that all traces of humanity were over-come by divinity. All the sheep's organs, after they were removed, had to have the blood washed out of them. This was the only way for them to be an acceptable pure sacrifice. There had to be no record of its own blood. Nothing of its DNA, or its own skin, its own covering remained. Then, its ribs were split and the heart was exposed for free access to the priest.

Just think. In the spirit, when Lawrence (or anyone else who surrenders to His divine will as a sacrifice and are patterned after Jesus Christ, made in His image) said "Yes" to the choice God gave him – God stripped, broke and grasped everything that made Lawrence, and stripped him, broke him and broke covenant in him to access the prize – his heart. Why? For fun?!

Ahhh! Now that one you would have to ask my son! I can only say that now he is married, stable, and about to graduate with a Master's Degree, with his wife in Seminary. Plus, they have a home free of strife, and all who enter it come out absolutely better and at peace. God has covered him with His righteousness, holiness, Divinity, with His heart; His will. He has covered him with Himself, returning him to a state before the fall of Adam. He, God, has covered Lawrence and Sarah with Himself. Now Lawrence is a spirit, has a soul, and lives in his body. He is in the order of God's original plan.

God created Adam, according to Genesis 1: 26, in His own image. God breathed into him and he became a Spirit being. Now Lawrence's spirit, by God through Christ in the breath of His Holy

Spirit, re-clothed Lawrence in His pure God-image form; Spirit, Soul and Body, total government in God's love. This, too, is a process and the agony of the original choice to be sacrificed has been forgotten as the glory of being married in purity, as two virgins, has been rewarded in manifested glory and rest. God, in Romans 8, also says that the suffering is not to be compared to the glory that is revealed!

12

LIVING OUT THE REIGN

I come home from the encounter at Jayme's in Colorado, where I have lived out a true "gutting" of all I have ever known. Both of us had surrendered, sacrificed all we had known, and patterned after Christ for the glory of being totally Christ's. I have already revealed the process of my surrender and sacrifice to be totally His, and the glory that followed. To understand the price of Lawrence's journey one must ask him.

I need to clarify something here. My second son, my husband's firstborn son, (he also has a daughter from a previous marriage whom I totally love as my own) is Stephen. In my own selfish addiction, Stephen was in a phase of addiction (drinking) that surpassed mine in volume and intensity. His actions and demeanor were unpredictable and violent. Sleeping for days and then up for 2 or 3 in a row, each time the whole household prayed it was the last time. With an angry father and an addicted mother, he learned well. One of the ways we would know he was on a bender was he only ate crackers and chewed ice. Kick him out? Sure: and his three children that lived with us for 3-4 days a week would be dragged from one filthy house to another in rough places. No thank you! Pleading prayers and horrible sinking ensued as he would succumb time and time again. (By the way, at the time of this writing he has been sober for almost two years. God and him; about to have another child, and supports his family quite well.)

So as I leave, I leave Lawrence and Sarah to deal with the effects of him too, and protecting the three grandbabies in case he was too rough. My children were dying in front of me and all they said was, "Yes, Mom, go." My God, I am so blessed! Stephen has now become the true sunny boy again able to light up the room with true light. His journey with his fiancé continues to test his will to trust God and yield. He has done this and does morning devotionals with his fiancé as they trust God together. Easy, no, worth it, ask him… To never need to have anything else control him but the Lord.

> *" Yes Mom. Go. "*

Stephen was not just a drunk or a loser in any way of the matter. He has three children, our grandbabies, and is the most heartwarming adult ever. When Stephen walks into a room he causes the whole room to smile. He is passionate about life, has a deep, deep faith and love of God, and has learned to be a great father, not just daddy and friend. He is divorced from his children's Mom and he lived with us. We had the babies three to four days a week. I helped out with cooking and childcare while my husband cleaned and drove everybody where they needed to go. My husband's was the only running vehicle most of the time. So, for Stephen to say, "Yes, Mom; leave for 5 weeks. I'll deal with Dad's moods, Lawrence's battles with Dad, the kids, the chaos and craziness," was unexpected. But Stephen was so supportive also.

"Go Mom." I know it sounds so simple, but it is so hard to express how much my boys gave me as they said, "Yes, Mom. Go." Stephen's smile lights up a room, and the life he brings everywhere he goes is felt by all. He has such a profound faith and trust in God that he just says, "Don't worry. God will work it out."

The birth of his first son Malachi is a great example. This is my son's firstborn son and labor for his (then) wife was long. Malachi, when he came forth, was not breathing. The cord was around his neck. The nurses went into action and took Malachi with limited chaos as he didn't cry. Stephen said later when I asked him, "Were you scared?" "No Mom, I knew God gave him to me and I wasn't scared for a moment." Great faith! Childlike faith! God said it, he believes it!

For such is the kingdom of God! And so he says, "Go, Mom. It will be okay. God's got this." There was no drama, no explanation or defense, just the same absolute faith that saved his son's life. God's got this!

Then there is my youngest son, Gary Jr. I knew, as I carried Gary Jr. in my belly, that he would be my last natural child. I knew. I babied him and kept him from responsibility, from growing up, and from life. He is very quiet, yet so intelligent, and because he is so quiet he was a living sacrifice for most of his older years. Stephen was "Sonny Boy", "Sports Boy", and all around everyone's friend. Gary is deep, thorough and straight to the point if pressed for an answer. He tells the truth, bar none. His heart is so big he is "Thunder heart", and the immense love he has with God is beyond words. He had moved to a place about an hour from our home three months before I left. He had been with his brother Lawrence for two years but this was the first time ever that he would leave home and go somewhere completely strange.

He moved out there to help with a presidential candidate in 2012 by managing media on the Internet. Yet, to me at that time, and still today, Gary Jr. represents such solid trust. Never to have been away from his family, out there on his own, facing his own shortcomings and fears. Lawrence and I could talk to him, and we did – along with his Pastor. Yet, it still was God and him when all is said and done, and He did this in the midst of a men's home, shelter and food ministry. To leave everything he had ever known, ever "babied", and ever loved, for God's voice. "Alone." Now that's a living sacrifice. As the encounters of this book and more unfolded, Gary Jr. is whom I would call. He would listen to me ramble on for hours about 'horses this' and 'eyeballs that' and flying scrolls that I could eat. Nothing I said fazed him. He would always say, "Good Mom. But to please

God, sometimes all you have to do is breathe." In the tsunami of life and death, as a person (me) who always "saw" everything, a statement like that would stop the frenzy.

Thunder heart: Don't mess with those he loves, Thunder heart: Able to hear God's voice clear through any noise and storm. Thunder heart; Quiet until the right conditions bring out a rending clasp, splitting the darkness of confusion and lies, in one swift BOOM! "Sometimes Mom, to please God, all you have to do is breathe."

Just breathe and be.

13

GOD'S TRIUMPH

It has been two years since this encounter. As I came home Lawrence said, "Save it Mom. I'll hear from God for myself." Stephen was in a cycle of great denial and chaos with drinking. And, Gary Jr. had been in-between jobs – just taking a break from "life", going to a park every day.

The place of Where Did You Put Your Reign continued to grow in me as all the effects of my sin and denial before being set free was still there at home. The biggest testimony, however, to God's government in my life was that I could walk without pain! As a matter of fact, I started climbing 900 foot "mountains" that were across the street from my home, spending hours upon hours with the Lord. Never again deciding which drug I needed just to be able to function on a daily basis! Nothing could separate me from His love. As the weeks unfolded I only became stronger, quieter and more confident. I began to take my son's lives to the court of the Kingdom of God. I stood as addiction (alcohol) in Stephen tried to stare me down in ugly demonstrations of emotional tolls in his life.

I stood.

Lawrence, who had raised his life to God in sacrifice, was not close to me at first. Why should He? Just like my other son with addiction's game, I had shown them well... then. I knew all of this, however, before I came home. I was not "out to save the world". I was 'in'; In God, In Abba Father, Lord and King. I had submitted to

Him, not as Savior only, but as King and Lord of my life. He, God, had already saved the world.

> *I can walk. I can think.*
> *I can climb. I can bend.*

He owned me completely.

I doubted nothing. Truly. I only waited as He showed me how to apply His kingship now to my home. "On earth as it is in heaven." Ah yes! Let me tell you. Now, the triumph of God!

I can walk. I can think. I can climb. I can bend. Oh, Lord, Yes, Lord, I am in awe! Even the knee that is a replacement bends! For the first time in ten years I kneel to praise You with tears of absolute amazement, running free in gratefulness! You have separated me unto Yourself, and pain, addiction, withdrawal and suffering no longer master me! You are my Lord. You are my King. You are my Majesty. And You are my Father. I do not need to be saved. You call me your "son", blood heir, joint heirs by the covenant of Your love whereby I cry, "Abba, Daddy, Father. All You have is mine. It is my inheritance and I am enjoying You more and more each and every day. The flesh has become a 'false prophet' as Your living oracles, words, live in me. Rejoicing, dancing and singing now consume me, to return unto You the very miracle that I am!" Song of Solomon 4 says, "Oh that you would come into your garden, (me) and eat its choicest fruits."

Lord, I now ask thee, "Sip so true, My wine, my cup." I offer myself to You. "Drink deeply now, taste and see! For I, my Lord, do taste like Thee! Full, robust, yet sweet and true; Taste, my King, I am a drink offering to You."

Abba, Father, Lord and King. As an encounter, He takes and savors a "sip" of me. He swishes in His cheeks the "body" of my being. Ahhh! Full-bodied is true, deep, yet sweet, strong and true! He licks my drink offering off of His lips. Truly we have saved the best wine for last! He now licks lovingly each droplet of me; now His.

My heart explodes in awesome bless. Abba Majesty states, "I'll have another cup of 'this'." We toast as we stare in the exchanging of truth. "Drink on, oh revelers of the palace. You can never make my lover disloyal to Me." He says. "Drink deeply of my love, oh precious one, for I know thou art Mine, Irrevocably Mine!

"Now, now it is time to pour you out onto a thirsty land..."

DR. CATHLEEN M. SCHMITT

EPILOGUE

It has been almost 11 months since returning home. All three of my sons are stable, sober, serving God in absolute joy. Did it just happen when I came home? No! The Lord truly gave me strength, focus, healing, joy and love. Also, the government of His kingdom, the law of Spirit of life in Christ Jesus has set me free from the law of sin and death. For the whole law is compiled within the one precept: You shall love your "neighbor" as yourself. I knew I am loved no matter what my surrounding said. Every day as I woke up I truly had to choose whether I would believe God, get up, walk, climb, pray, sing. Or believe the lie that would try to sneak in: "Oh, you're a bit sore today, Just rest. Oh, you're tired today. You need sleep. Hey, Isn't that a new cramp in your foot?" Yet, each day I will take communion, remembering Him and what He did. Remembering His song, His stare, His word that caused me to walk in the first place!

His love, nothing can separate me from! Nothing! Yet I must choose to think and pursue His love. Choose? Hah! He woos me! And remember, in the heavenly court I am not guilty in my flesh! This was a discipline at first, empowered by the Holy Spirit. As I turned my thoughts to what is pure and lovely and a good report, it is what returned unto me in my body. Many days in the beginning my "flesh" would cry out with imagined pains. Yet Truth, the absolute truth of my being in court, in the Law of life in Christ and in love wins out.

My God! To feel again without pills! To feel anything original outside of a worldly influence is so amazing! Never to have to decide every morning what pill to take just to sit up! Oh, it became so easy to choose to remember Him, to think on Him. Yet it is a choice none-the-less. Four to six hours a day I soak and dwell and be and breathe in Him. Is it necessary to "waste" so much time? I found that the more I thought on Him and walked and talked, the more I wanted to be with Him.

On August 15, 2012, I canceled a surgery for a complete knee replacement. It had taken two years to get insurance approval and authorization for the surgery. It took Abba, Father, Lord and King one moment to say, "And now, Cathy, you may ask pain to leave, for you love Me beyond your own need." I have a right to be loved and whole! It is God's law! I must choose to believe, and then, as has happened now, it is no longer a choice but normal! The Lord showed me His inseparable eternal love by His death and resurrection for me! When I chose to be loved and believed His love for me, when I knew nothing I could do could make Him love me less, and nothing I could do could cause Him to love me more... There was no more fight left in me, just a choice. "Cathy, you are worthy to be loved." How then can I not spend the rest of my days returning His heart back to Him?

Does everything go perfectly? No! But the things on earth do not define who I am or dictate my rights. I have been surrounded by sheer hatred really, and the Lord and King of my life, love, God is love, has caused a standard that does not respond to something I am no longer a part of. In fact, for the understanding of God's governing law of life in Christ Jesus, I was kept in a situation that cursed me each day. A situation that looked for wrong in me, yelled, demanded and cursed me really. Situations being as they were I took actions to have this person removed legally, and In Ephesians it tells us that "We wrestle not against flesh and blood, but against principalities, powers, rulers of darkness of the world and against spiritual wickedness in high places. WHEREFORE put on the whole armor of God that you may withstand in the evil day, AND HAVING DONE ALL, TO STAND. STAND therefore having your loins gird up with truth, having the breastplate of righteousness, your feet shod with the preparation of the gospel of peace, and above all, taking the shield of faith wherewith you will be able to quench ALL the fiery darts of the wicked. Then the helmet of salvation and the sword of the Spirit, which is the word of God, praying in the Spirit and watching in perseverance." (KJV, Ephesians 6: 12-18, emphasis mine)

So, I do not give attention to rantings of enemy, flesh and man as I move out in God's supply for me. "Thus you are nullifying and making void and of no effect [the authority of] the Word of God through your tradition, which you [in turn] hand on. And many things of this kind you are doing." (AMP, Mark 7: 13)

With every fiber of my being, I give this person all that I have but it was never enough. Then I truly realized that God has a journey for him – for him. I stopped praying because I knew God prayed, God intercedes, and God has finished, in him, what He started. I had spent so much time as the pious, good, loving victim, just praying until something happens. I nearly died in my lack of faith in a true, kind, loving God that does not allow sustained abuse of any kind.

It is a lie and I was afraid to be alone to face the horrors of abuse, rape, molestation and drugs. Pain needs a partner. Fear and Control are always ready to marry in. I listened as he would say, "You'll be put into a nursing home." (I was so broken in my body that it was a fact.) "No one will want you. You're too much to take care of. You will die alone." Well, I tell you now in hindsight, maybe I would have been in a nursing home, but God is God and all that means is in His healing love I would have taken the whole nursing home with me as He healed me!

But I settled, and Fear married Pain as sure as I married my husband.

"Don't you have authority over that spirit, Cathy?" Yes, yes, I do. But, I do not have authority over the free will of the man who has a choice, as do all of us, to believe and change. Or who states, "This is how I am. Oh well, deal with it," and be left behind in the traditions of men. I am not God. God gave man free will. I have the right of worth and love to now say, "Enough!" I am above and not beneath; above in love, not a victim. I am as victorious as those who chose life, my three sons, who saw miraculous healings in their own lives. Healing from addictions, fears, isolation and ignorance. They now live in marriage, joy, true fatherhood, governmental positions, sobriety, and in God's journey for each of them.

This past Mother's Day was the first Mother's day ever, EVER, I could own being a mother. They, my sons, all of them, now turn to me for prayer, insight and encouragement. They do this at times because they can. However, the greatest joy is seeing them all share with me what God said, for them, for their circumstances, for their lives. What an amazing transformation, truly for those who chose life! God said, "I set before you this day life and death, therefore choose life that ye may live!" (KJV, Deuteronomy 30: 15)

I am released now from the constant attention and time this caused me. The Lord says, "Cathy! About face! About My face! Turn your thoughts wholly to Me. He will not love you. He cannot." For thirty-two years I was not perfect by any means, but I loved! Oh, how I loved! I always could and always did. It is my greatest weapon and yet my greatest "weakness" at the time.

In my husband's perspective I am never good enough, thin enough, kind enough, repentant enough... The promise of "It's the pills," he would say. "It's the medicine's side effects that make you think I am being mean. I'm not really. It's the side effects of the pills." I could not tell if he was correct, so I would seek the Lord even more to be "good enough" over the effects of the drugs.

"If you only could be sober you'd see," he would say. "We will go driving and hiking and live our golden years as we should." I so believed it was my fault. I really did. As my body was racked in the need for a knee replacement and wrapped in pain's fog, only one voice was clear; Abba, Father, Lord and King Jesus. Yet still, the Lord showed me my responsibility in the matter.

I had believed that he would change for so long that to give up, well... Each time I would think of it, I'd say in a small corner of my being, "It worked. See? He changed. He does love me. I am good enough now." Yet, as God led me to be wholly His, He asked me, as I prepared to divorce myself from this way of living, "What will you lose, really Cathy? A dream? A fantasy? No, Cathy, you were not right. You were afraid, afraid of feeling your own inner child who was molested, afraid to feel. Feelings kill, so keep on believing in him and defending him. Continue to defend the place inside of you that was so bad, unlovable and Judas. The place that said, 'You Cath, need to be punished in some way'. Really truly you believed you were unlovable. What about 'Love bears all things, believes all things, hopes all things... love never fails?' (KJV, 1 Corinthians 13) I am Love!"

God says. "I bore it all in my Son. I am your hope. I never fail for those who believe Me. I didn't fail you! I didn't fail your boys, but you cannot force someone to love you by being good enough! No! There still remains a choice, free will, and your husband has all the 'right' in the world to choose not to love you. It is a choice, which is my highest gift to all mankind, to be able to choose individually, to love or not to love. To seek me (love), or stay self-focused. Does this make him evil or bad?"

Now, God says, "This is where it is my business. I alone try the heart of a man. I alone am God. I AM GOD." So here's the real question I ask, "Where did I put this pain? The pain of being wrong, of being so wrong it injured and hurt others in its focus? Is everything you trusted a lie? A waste of years? A waste of life? And, where do the 'I'm so sorry. I'm so sorry, sons, for the trauma and abandonment and, and, and...' Where do the 'I'm sorry for the victims of what was done' begin in this awakening of my heart? My heart is no longer numb.' Great!? Is it all wasted time?"

"No, my dear daughter. It was and still is the journey of a heart separated from Me and its home. See, Pain was much more familiar to you than I was at the time. At least you knew the outcome of the situation and cycle of abuse; yell, scream, cry, sorry, help, peace, yell, scream, cry, sorry, help, peace... This knowing pattern in a world where you could not trust much. This pattern was more familiar than trusting the unknown, of loving Me, trusting and hoping in Me. It, too, is a form of control. 'They will see how 'bad' he is, how awful he's been and what a great martyr I've been, how strong I am.' No Cathy, They just wonder when you will wake up and who in their right mind would ever stay in such conditions. See, you cannot be good enough through any action by yourself. You're good enough because I made you good, and I am good, and I am love, and you're good enough to be loved because I am God. Remember I love you in order for Me to show you this again I remind you that when, in your very nature (Ephesians 2) you were unable to love Me. I, Cathy, placed you in My Son, raised you up and seated you in the heavenly realms! By grace, so that no one, not even you, can boast!

"Where did I put My pain and My reign? In My Son, in My love, and I buried it once and for all in the blood and raised you up to rule in love through Me! Hear and see Me calling true; 'Come up here. Come up here.'"

And so I do...

In Psalms, it states, "Make a joyful noise unto the lord. Come into His presence with singing!" (KJV, Psalms 100: 2) No longer do I seek to 'pull Him down here.' No, He says. "Come up here," by song, by joy, by love. "Come up here on your rightful seat in the heavenly realm, (sphere) so you can see with Me how small the worldly matters are compared to Me! Come up here! I already came down in my Son to bring you up with Me, to see, to be, to breathe, to rule from the heavenlies!"

I am captivated once again. I absorb His invitation to "come up here into My being" and inside of His heart, inside of Jesus, inside His pierced side now whole, wholly one in Him. Jesus brings me inside Him, before the Father, His Majesty, the Lord and King. Father smiles as the radiance of His Son, now complete with creation (me, us) inside. As it was in the beginning, "Let us make man in our image and let him have dominion over all the earth." (KJV, Genesis 1: 26) Father smiles. Truly on earth as it is in heaven, His kingdom has come, His will has been done, creation, delivered from evil. Father is seated on the throne, radiant. He looks at His complete Son, pats His legs, smiles and nods His head. Jesus smiles in return, turns around, backs up into His Father's legs, and with all creation fully inside, sits down into the Father, returning thus my love, all love, from whence it came.

"For God so loved the world (me), He gave His only begotten Son, that whosoever would believe in Him would not die, but have eternal life. (KJV, John 3:16)

"In the beginning," God spoke into the dark void of my life and said, "Let there be light." (Genesis 1:2) And it (I) was very, very, very good! For there is NO PAIN, NO SHAME, OR NO GAME so deep that God's love is not deeper still!

God sustains me, open door
His revelations, I implore
Spirit fills my inner core,
Christ divine within.
No questions unanswered when rules aren't norm
We're flying past this human form
To live, to breathe revelation's storm,
In the beauty of God's face.
Holy Spirit dwells in human flesh,
No chance for mortal fortresses
My mind, my will transformed by His

Heaven here on earth!

EPILOGUE 2

Two years have flown by and they have been the best two years of my life. As I briefly mentioned before, all three of my sons are now amazing and serving God. Lawrence and his wife Sarah had their first child, a son, and have been ordained as Pastors.

Stephen awaits the arrival of his baby girl in September and has never returned to addiction
again.

Gary Jr. has moved in with his brother, working as a security guard. All of them had to adjust to see if what happened to Mom (me) would last. Anger, especially deep in Gary Jr. has now become trust as we build a mother/son relationship; not a pal on whom I dump all my processing. He preaches with his brother when our Pastor leaves for various duties. He has allowed God to heal the abandonment and selfish places I exhibited during most of his life. He was always quiet, so he must be okay. Just don't ask too much or he will answer! Now he is focused, working hard and the Thunder in his heart no longer scares me. I ask and ask a lot, and I can finally hear him. He truly has the love of the Father Lord which is deep and faithful. He is a man of integrity and truth.

I am about to graduate with a Doctorate in Pastoral Ministries, with a Masters in Biblical Counseling. The date of August of 2014 seemed impossible for my graduation and now it is upon me.

I truly know my life has just begun.

To God be the Glory great things He has done!

[1]Axonal Damage in Traumatic Brain Injury

DOUGLAS H. SMITH and DAVID F. MEANEY
Departments of Neurosurgery (DHS) and Bioengineering (DFM)
University of Pennsylvania
Philadelphia, Pennsylvania

[2]The Truth About Oxycodone Withdrawal
http://www.novusdetox.com/oxycodone-withdrawal-symptoms.php

[3]The Truth About Oxycodone Withdrawal
http://www.novusdetox.com/oxycodone-withdrawal-symptoms.php

Made in the USA
Lexington, KY
26 September 2018